Language, Ontology, Terminology and Knowledge Structures Workshop (LOTKS 2017)

Montpellier, France
19 September 2017

Editors:

Francesca Frontini
Larisa Grcic Simeunovic
Spela Vintar

Fahad Khan
Artemis Parvisi

ISBN: 978-1-5108-5287-7

Proceedings of the
Language, Ontology, Terminology and
Knowledge Structures Workshop
(LOTKS 2017)

Held in conjunction with the
12th International Conference on Computational Semantics (IWCS)

19 September 2017
Montpellier (France)

Editors:

**Francesca Frontini, Larisa Grčić Simeunović,
Špela Vintar, Fahad Khan, Artemis Parvisi**

Workshop Organizers

Francesca Frontini - Laboratoire Praxiling Université Paul-Valéry Montpellier 3, France
Larisa Grčić Simeunović - University of Zadar, Croatia
Anas Fahad Khan - Istituto di Linguistica Computazionale "A. Zampolli" - CNR, Italy
Artemis Parvizi - Oxford University Press, UK
Špela Vintar   - University of Ljubljana, Slovenia

Workshop Programme Committee

Amparo Alcina - Universitat Jaume I
Nathalie Aussenac-Gilles - IRIT CNRS
Caroline Barriere - CRIM
Andrea Bellandi - Istituto di Linguistica Computazionale "A. Zampolli", CNR, Italy
Carmen Brando - École des hautes études en sciences sociales (EHESS)
Sandra Bringay - LIRMM
Paul Buitelaar - Insight Centre for Data Analytics, National University of Ireland Galway
Elena Cabrio - Université Côte d'Azur, CNRS, Inria, I3S, France
Elena Cardillo - Institute for Informatics and Telematics, Italian National Council of Research
Philipp Cimiano - Bielefeld University
Francesco Corcoglioniti - Fondazione Bruno Kessler
Béatrice Daille - Laboratoire d'Informatique Nantes Atlantique (LINA)
Angelo Mario Del Grosso - Istituto di Linguistica Computazionale "A. Zampolli", CNR, Italy
Jean-Gabriel Ganascia - Pierre and Marie Curie University, LIP6
Aldo Gangemi - Université Paris 13 & CNR-ISTC
Eric Gaussier - LIG-UJF
Emiliano Giovannetti - Istituto di Linguistica Computazionale "A. Zampolli", CNR, Italy
Jorge Gracia - Ontology Engineering Group, Universidad Politécnica de Madrid
Ulrich Heid - IMS, University of Stuttgart
Agata Jackiewicz - Université Paul-Valéry (Montpellier 3)
Caroline Jay - University of Manchester
Marie-Claude L'Homme - Observatoire de linguistique Sens-Texte (OLST)
Pilar León Araúz - University of Granada
John P. Mccrae - National University of Ireland, Galway
Monica Monachini - Istituto di Linguistica Computazionale "A. Zampolli", CNR, Italy
María Navas-Loro - Ontology Engineering Group, Universidad Politécnica de Madrid
Mojca Pecman - Paris Diderot Paris 7
Fabio Rinaldi - Institute of Computational Linguistics, University of Zurich
Christophe Roche - Université de Savoie
Mathieu Roche - Cirad, TETIS
Laurent Romary - INRIA & HUB-ISDL
Gilles Sérasset - Université Joseph Fourier, Grenoble
Armando Stellato - University of Rome, Tor Vergata
Markel Vigo - University of Manchester
Adam Wyner - University of Aberdeen

Workshop Programme

Exploratory Analysis for Ontology Learning from Social Events on Social Media Streaming in Spanish

Enrique Valeriano
Facultad de Ciencias e Ingeniería
Pontificia Universidad Católica del Perú
enrique.valeriano@pucp.pe

Arturo Oncevay-Marcos
Departamento de Ciencias e Ingeniería
Pontificia Universidad Católica del Perú
arturo.oncevay@pucp.edu.pe

Abstract

The problem of event analysis in Spanish social media streaming is that of difficulty on automatically processing the data as well as obtaining the most relevant information, such as mentioned by Derczynski et al. (2015). An event is defined as a real world occurrence that takes place in a specific time and space; Atefeh and Khreich (2013) identifies these occurrences by the entities that took part on it as well as the activities done in it. This project focuses on researching about the viability of modeling these events as ontologies using an automatic approach for entities and relationships extraction in order to obtain relevant information about the event in case. Spanish data from Twitter was used as a study case and tested with the developed application.

1   Introduction

According to Lobzhanidze et al. (2013), globalization and the increased use of social networks has made it possible for news and events related information to be propagated in a much faster manner to every part of the world. It is in this context that event analysis is the most relevant since, as Valkanas and Gunopulos (2013) mention, now there is more data available to study and analyze than ever before.

An event is defined as a real world occurrence that takes place in a specific time and space; Atefeh and Khreich (2013) identifies these occurrences by the entities that took part on it as well as the activities done in it. Events will be the main study object in this paper and, more specifically, event data in Spanish obtained from Twitter will be used to test the different methods and techniques exposed on each Section.

In order to effectively analyze events there are two steps that need to be taken into consideration as mentioned in Kumbla (2016): (1) event data acquisition, and (2) event data processing.

The first step is the one that benefits the most by social media streaming since more data is available, though one of the downsides to this is that the data is usually not ready to be used right away and most of the times a preprocessing step needs to happen. This step is further explained on section Section 3.

The second step will be the main focus on this paper since the biggest problem on event data analysis in Spanish is this one. In particular, automatic approaches for entities and relationships extraction will be presented on Section 4.

The remainder of this paper is organized as follows. In Section 2 some relevant related work is exposed. Later, in Section 3 the event acquisition process is further expanded upon. The ontology structure used for the events representation as well as the algorithms employed in order to obtain entities and relationships between these are further explained on Section 4. Section 5 introduces a simple application developed in order to make use of the algorithms and techniques mentioned on the previous sections. On section 6 we compare the results obtained with manually created ontologies and obtain precision and recall values for each case. Finally, concluding remarks are provided in Section 7.

2   Related Work

In Al-Smadi and Qawasmeh (2016) an unsupervised approach for event extraction from Arabic tweets is discussed. Entities appearing in the data are linked to corresponding entities found on Wikipedia and DBpedia through an ontology based knowledge base. The entities from the data are extracted based on rules related to the Arabic language.

In Derczynski et al. (2015) a comparative evaluation of different NER is done based on three different datasets. Also, some common challenges or errors when handling data from Twitter are presented as well as methods for reducing microblog noise through pre-processing such as language identification, POS-tagging and normalization.

In Ilknur et al. (2011) a framework for learning relations between entities in Twitter is presented. This framework allows for entities as well as entity types or topics to be detected, which results in a graph connecting semantically enriched resources to their respective entities. Then relation discovery strategies are employed to detect pair of entities that have a certain type of relationship in a specific period of time.

In Raimond and Abdallah (2007) an event ontology is described. This model also contains some key characteristics such as place, location, agents and products. On the other hand, event-subevent relationships are used to build the related ontologies. This model was developed for the Center for Digital Music and tested by structuring proceedings and concert descriptions.

Finally, an ontology model for events is proposed in which entities are extracted using the CMU tweet analyzer and relationships are inferred from Wikipedia, DBpedia and Web data. This approach also uses a POS-tagging step in order to obtain the initial set of entities to process.

3   Event data acquisition

3.1   Data retrieval

As it was mentioned before, nowadays there are numerous avenues for event data acquisition. For this paper Twitter was chosen as the social network to use for retrieving data since this data is easily available and a good amount of it is related to events of different categories.

Twitter's REST API was used in order to retrieve data related to these events:

1. Australian Open: 2217 tweets from 21/01/2017 to 30/01/2017

2. March against corruption in Peru: 1493 tweets from 11/02/2017 to 20/02/2017

3. Complaints about new toll in Puente Piedra: 3882 tweets from 08/01/2017 to 18/01/2017

Each dataset had a file per day with all the tweets from the day and contained only the text that represents a tweet per line.

3.2   Preprocessing

With the raw data ready to be used, the preprocessing step followed. The sequence followed is exposed below:

1. Removing punctuation and unicode only characters except written accents.

2. Tokenizing the tweets for easier use in Section 4.

Each tokenized tweet also contains a reference to the original, unprocessed tweet, which will be used on Section 5.

4 Event data processing

4.1 Ontology learning overview

Ontology learning is defined by Cimiano (2006) as the automatic acquisition of a domain model from some dataset. In this paper we focus on applying ontology learning techniques for data represented as text.

Cimiano points towards two main approaches for ontology learning:

1. Machine learning

2. Statistical approach

Statistical based algorithms are further discussed on Sections 4.3 and 4.4.

4.2 Ontology structure

Before we start using different techniques in order to populate an ontology or to learn entities and relationships from the data that was retrieved previously, an ontology structure had to be defined.

The ontology structure that we define will point us towards different techniques depending on the information that must be retrieved to populate this particular structure. Therefore, the proposed ontology structure in this paper is defined on Figure 1.

Figure 1: Entity structure

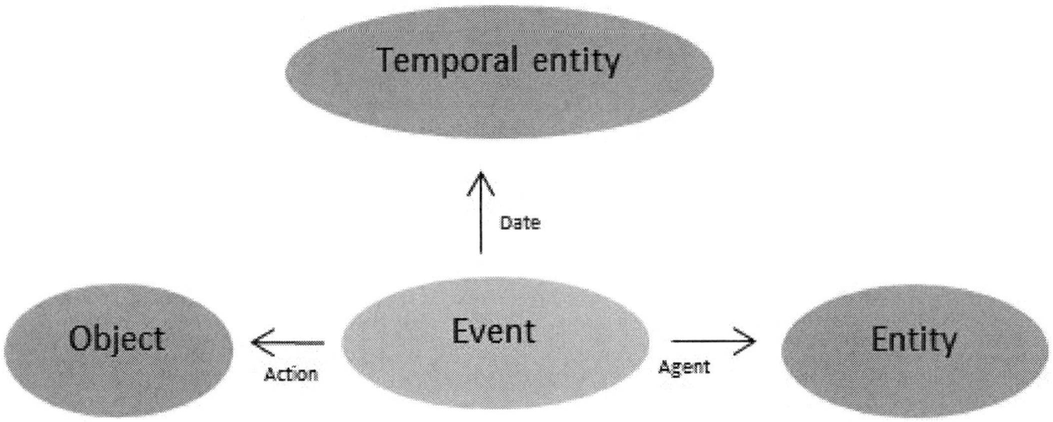

The ontology will be populated by such triples composed of (Entity, Temporal entity, object). Where Entity denotes a subject that interacts in the event, Temporal entity refers to the date when the particular activity takes place and object is the recipient of the activity.

4.3 Entities extraction

This was one of the main points of interest and research on this paper, how to select the most representative entities for the event in order to not overwhelm people analyzing the results but also to not present too little or irrelevant information.

In order to achieve this, two initial tools for entity retrieval were tested:

1. Stanford NER: The Stanford NER used with a trained Spanish model from late 2016 was used in order to retrieve persons, entities and organizations and group them all together as entities.

2. UDPipe: UDPipe allows to parse text in order to obtain the grammatical categories of the words in each sentence, as well as the syntactic dependencies or syntactic tree that envelops the whole sentence. The entities are obtained from the grammatical category **PROPN**.

These two approaches were then implemented and tested with each dataset and a manual comparison was made between the entities that each approach captured.

The results showed that, while the Stanford NER worked really well in the case where the tweets were news related or had a more formal undertone, such as in the case of the Australian Open, it failed to find a lot of basic entities in the other two datasets where the data was more unstructured as one would very likely find when working on social streaming. Also, the Stanford NER has heavily influenced by correct capitalization and punctuation, whereas UDPipe wasn't influenced by these factors as much.

Because of this, UDPipe was chosen as the main initial entity extraction tool moving forward.

After having a set of initial entities, further processing steps were taken to ensure a better result.

4.3.1   Entity clustering

Entity clustering was done on two stages. First, an algorithm for entity clustering was devised based on two metrics:

1. Normalized frequency of two entities appearing in a single tweet: The frequency of appearance between two specific entities in tweets.

2. Average Entity to entity distance in a tweet (i.e. in the sentence "Nadal venció a Federer", if both Nadal and Federer are identified as entities, they would have a distance of 3 for this tweet)

A threshold of 0.125 was set as the minimum normalized frequency for a pair of entities and a minimum average Entity to Entity distance of 1.65. These two values were set based on experimentation with the resulting clustered entities from each dataset.

After that, an approach based on Levenshtein distance (minimum amount of additions, replacements or deletions needed to turn a word into another) was employed, where two entities were clustered together if their distance was more than 0.9 times the length of the longest entity from the two. An example of this distance can be seen on Figure 2.

Figure 2: Example of Levenshtein distance

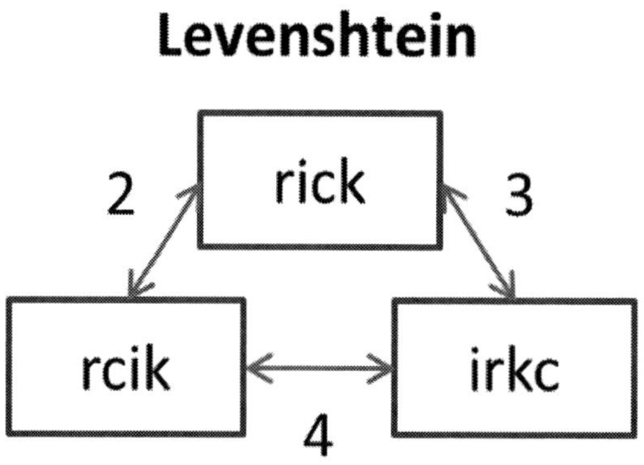

By applying this, resulting clusters such as the ones shown on Figure 3 were obtained.

Figure 3: Resulting clusters for the Australian Open case

```
australian:australianopen,australian,australianopen,open,australia,
nadal:rafael,nadal,rafaelnadal,
andy:andy,murray,
serena:williams,serenawilliams,serena,wlliams,
federer:federe,roger,rogerfederer,federer,
grand:slam,grand,
mischa:mischa,zverev,mischazverev,
```

4.3.2 Formal Context Analysis (FCA)

FCA is one of the approaches for entity extraction detailed on Cimiano (2006). It is the one that garners the most focus on this book as the main set-theoretical approach based on verb-subject components.

This approach is based on obtaining the formal context for a specific domain or dataset and then proceed to use it to create a hierarchy ontology.

An example of how a formal context would look for a tourism domain knowledge can be seen on Table 1.

Table 1: Example of a tourism domain knowledge as a formal context Cimiano (2006)

	bookable	rentable	rideable
hotel	X		
apartment	X	X	
bike	X	X	X
excursion	X		
trip	X		

In this paper we use the created formal contexts to discriminate between entities based on three metrics:

$$Conditional(n, v) = P(n, v) = \frac{f(n, v)}{f(v)} \tag{1}$$

$$PMI(n, v) = log_2 \frac{P(n|v)}{P(n)} \tag{2}$$

$$Resnik(n, v) = SR(v) * P(n|v) \tag{3}$$

Where:

1. f(n,v) => Frequency of apparition of entity n with verb v

2. f(v) => Frequency of apparition of verb v with any entity

And:

$$SR(v) = \sum_n P(n|v) * log_2 \frac{P(n|v)}{P(n)} \tag{4}$$

A threshold of 0.1 as a minimum value is set for all of the three aforementioned metrics (Conditional, PMI and Resnik weights), meaning that the (entity,verb) pairs that not surpass this threshold for any of the three metrics are pruned.

4.4   Relationships extraction

In this subsection UDPipe is also used in order to extract the syntactic dependencies, in particular, the focus is to obtain 'dobj' and 'iobj' objects, which refer to direct and indirect object respectively, and then obtain the root verb they stem from.

By doing this a verb can be linked to each object and furthermore, the entities related to verb, which were obtained from the Formal Context, can be linked to each object.

Doing this allows us to add activities for each entity, as well as create a relationship between two entities where one of them appears as an object in the action of another.

5   Visualization

A desktop application was developed in order to allow for easier visualization of both the ontology and the resulting activities that each entity participated in, as well as the activities that create a relationship between two particular entities.

Figure 4: Timeline for the entity rafaelnadal

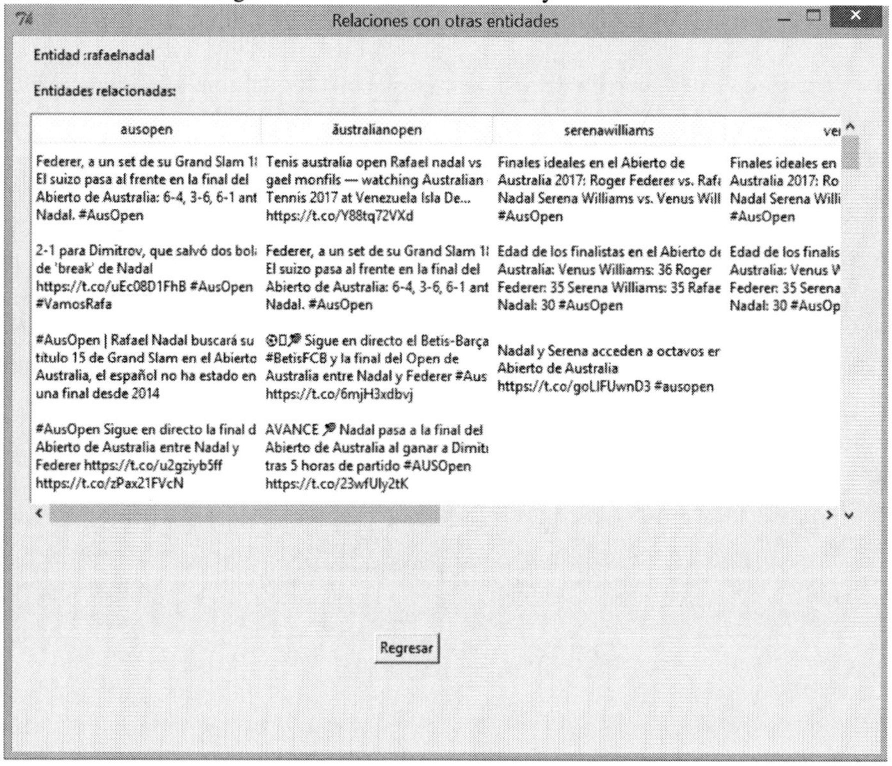

On Figure 4 a timeline was given for the entity rafaelnadal on the Australian Open case, where each day has tweets that represent activities that were extracted from the dataset.

6   Verification

In order to verify the approach applied for ontology extraction, we manually created ontologies for each test case where the most relevant entities and relationships are specified based on investigation related to these cases, these ontologies can be seen on Figures 5, 6 and 7.

These ontologies were then presented to colleagues with more profound knowledge on each of the events for validation and were redone based on their feedback until they were accepted by them.

Figure 5: Ontology created for the Australian Open case

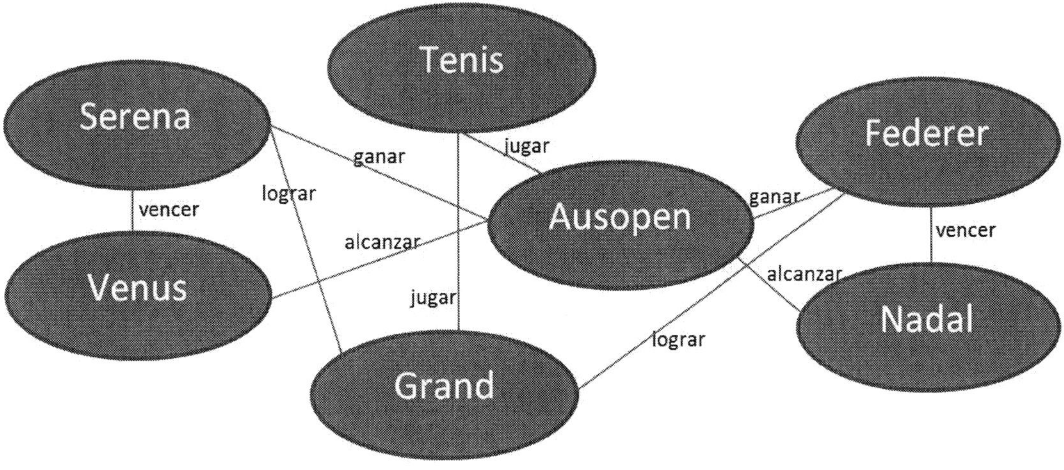

Figure 6: Ontology created for the Puente Piedra's toll case

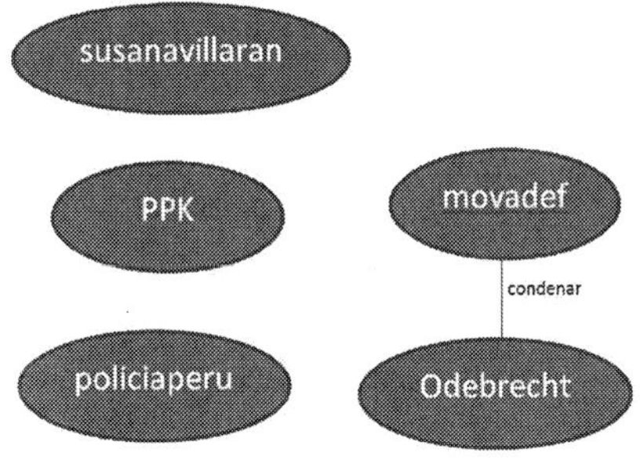

Figure 7: Ontology created for the March against the Corruption case

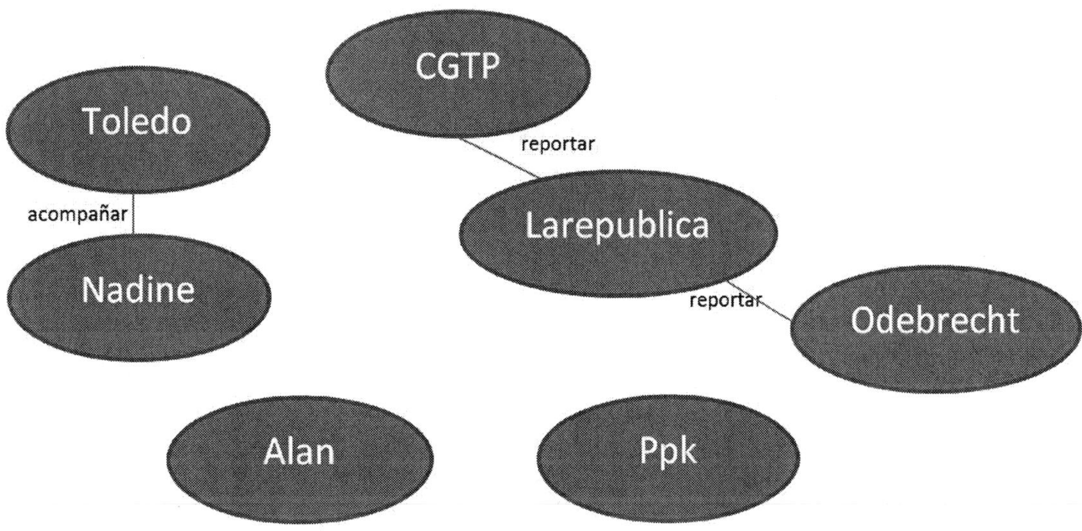

From these ontologies we obtained precision and recall values for both entities and relationships for each case. These can be seen on Tables 2, 3 and 4:

Table 2: Metrics for the Australian Open case

Analyzed parameter	Metric	Value
Entities	Precision	0.875
Entities	Recall	1.0
Relationships	Precision	0.952
Relationships	Recall	1.0

Table 3: Metrics for the Puente Piedra's toll case

Analyzed parameter	Metric	Value
Entities	Precision	0.556
Entities	Recall	1.0
Relationships	Precision	0.333
Relationships	Recall	1.0

Table 4: Metrics for the March against Corruption case

Analyzed parameter	Metric	Value
Entities	Precision	0.467
Entities	Recall	1.0
Relationships	Precision	0.333
Relationships	Recall	0.667

The main point of interest in these metrics lies on the precision, where the precision on the Australian Open case in quite higher than on the other two cases. From further inspection on the corresponding data we could infer that this was the case because a big part of the tweets for the Australian Open where either formal tweets made by users representing news outlets or by the players themselves. As for the other two cases, most of the tweets where a mix of news and discussion from common people about these events.

7 Conclusions and future work

We conclude that, while the methods exposed on this paper work good enough on cases such as the Australian Open one, there is still work to be done when the general public is more engaged on the event such as the cases of the Puente Piedra toll and the March against the corruption.

This paper's aim was to give a foundation and a initial stage of exploratory analysis on social media streaming in Spanish by using ontologies, after which future work could be based upon in order to expand the knowledge in the ontologies or use this analysis together with an event detection system in order to be able to both detect and analyze events in real time.

References

Al-Smadi, M. and O. Qawasmeh (2016). Knowledge-based approach for event extraction from arabic tweets. *International Journal of Advanced Computer Science and Applications 7*, 483–490.

Atefeh, F. and W. Khreich (2013). A survey of techniques for event detection in twitter. *Computational Intelligence 0*(0).

Cimiano, P. (2006). *Ontology Learning and Population from Text Algorithms, Evaluation and Applications*. 223 Spring Street, New York, NY 10013: Springer Science+Business Media.

Derczynski, L., D. Maynard, G. R., M. v.E., and G. G. (2015). Analysis of named entity recognition and linking for tweets. *Information Processing and Management 51*, 32–49.

Ilknur, C., A. F., and H. G. (2011). Learning semantic relations between entities in twitter. *Information Processing and Management 51*, 32–49.

Kumbla, S. (2016). Fast data: Powering real-time big data.

Lobzhanidze, A., W. Zeng, P. Gentry, and A. Taylor (2013). Mainstream media vs. social media for trending topic prediction - an experimental study. *Consumer Communications and Networking Conference (CNNC)*, 729–732.

Raimond, Y. and S. Abdallah (2007). The event ontology.

Valkanas, G. and D. Gunopulos (2013). Event detection from social media data.

Creating a gold standard corpus for terminological annotation from online forum data

Anna Hätty	Simon Tannert	Ulrich Heid
Robert Bosch GmbH	University of Stuttgart	University of Hildesheim
`Anna.Haetty@`	`simon.tannert@`	`heid@`
`de.bosch.com`	`ims.uni-stuttgart.de`	`uni-hildesheim.de`

Abstract

We present ongoing work on a gold standard annotation of German terminology in an inhomogeneous domain. The text basis is thematically broad and contains various registers, from expert text to user-generated data taken from an online discussion forum. We identify issues related with these properties, and show our approach how to model the domain. Futhermore, we present our approach to handle multiword terms, including discontinuous ones. Finally, we evaluate the annotation quality.

1 Introduction

Terms are linguistic expressions typical of specialized domains (Kagueura and Umino (1996)). In this work, texts from the domain of do-it-yourself instructions and reports (DIY) are chosen as basis for a gold standard annotation of terminology. The DIY domain is characterized by a broad range of topics, and our text corpus in addition covers several registers. This results in the presence of term candidates with different status and poses a challenge to the annotation approach. We describe our way to model the degree of termhood and the relation of multiword terms to their variants. The model serves as a basis to define rules to limit an outgrowth of term candidates. The gold standard is intended to be a reference dataset for automatic term extraction. Such a system has to cope with heterogeneous domains, with morphologically related term variants as well as with variants emerging from the different styles present in the text corpus.

In the following, our domain and annotation approach are positioned on the map of existing term annotation work. In section 3, we describe how the text basis is chosen to ensure that it is representative of the DIY domain. In section 4, we describe the annotation procedure and address the challenges that arise from the selected domain and registers. Finally, our annotation is evaluated, and we interpret systematic divergences between annotators. We conclude in section 5.

2 Related Work

Existing Benchmark Datasets for Term Extraction   There exists a range of terminology benchmark datasets which vary in the specificity of their topic, their definition of termhood and writing styles. Well-known datasets are the **Genia** (Kim et al. (2003)) and the **CRAFT corpus** (Bada et al. (2012)) with term annotations in the biomedical domain. Genia contains 2000 MEDLINE abstracts with almost 100,000 annotations by two domain experts. CRAFT consists of 67 biomedical journal articles of various biological domains (plus unpublished articles) with more than 100,000 concept annotations. **ACL RD-TEC** (Handschuh and QasemiZadeh (2014)) is a gold standard in the domain of computational linguistics. It consists of 10,922 ACL conference papers published between 1965 and 2006. From those more than 83, 000 term candidates have been extracted and evaluated; 22,000 candidates are annotated as valid and 61,000 as invalid terms by one annotator. An extension is **ACL RD-TEC 2.0** (QasemiZadeh and Schumann (2016)), a further annotation of 300 ACL abstracts with a broad subclassification of the terms.

corpora	ACL 1.0	ACL 2.0	B/C	Bitter	TTC	Genia	Craft	our approach
breadth	**	**	**/*	**	**	*	**	***
registers	*	*	*	*	**	*	*	***
token-based	-	+	+	+	-	+	+	+
guidelines	broad	broad	mid/strict	broad	mid	strict	strict	mid

Table 1: Comparison of terminology gold standards

Bernier-Colborne and Drouin (2014) (B/C) analysed three textbooks on automotive engineering. In addition to the annotation, they assign attributes to the terms (e.g. for acronyms or multiwords) and mark orthographic variants. Other reference sets consist of bilingual term lists to evaluate machine translation. In the **TTC project** (Loginova et al. (2012)), a list of term candidates is generated with a term extraction tool and then further evaluated by experts. In the **BitterCorpus** (Arcan et al. (2014)), terms are annotated in texts from KDE and GNOME documentation corpora. In the following, we compare the reference datasets wrt. the size of their domain, the registers represented and the underlying annotation approach (see also Table 1).

Domain. The reference datasets differ wrt. the breadth of the topics covered. Genia's domain is very narrow, it is specialized to biological reactions concerning transcription factors in human blood cells. The texts are crawled on the basis of three seed terms. With Bernier-Colborne and Drouin, the topic is automotive engineering as presented in three textbooks for lay people. For CRAFT and ACL RD-TEC, journal and conference articles have been taken from a wide range of subtopics in their respective domains, and different research areas of the domains are included in the text basis. The same holds for the BitterCorpus: In the GNOME and KDE manuals, a range of topics, such as the user interface, settings, the internet connection or information about hardware are addressed. All these corpora have clearly defined content since the extraction basis is hand-selected. This does not hold for the TTC texts, which are retrieved by a thematic web crawler; unexpected text can thus occur in the corpus. The topics of our own data are even more open: The DIY domain is broad in itself, and as the texts come from different sources, the variety of topics even increases. Several slightly off-topic texts are part of the text basis.

Register. Most of the gold standard corpora are homogeneous wrt. register. They either consist of scientific articles (Genia, CRAFT, ACL RD-TEC 1.0 and 2.0) or of instruction texts: The three expert-to-lay textbooks for automotive engineering might differ slightly from author to author, but nevertheless have the explanatory style of textbooks. Finally, the KDE and the GNOME documentation follow the style of online manuals. Different registers only occur in the crawled text of TTC. In our work, we deliberately chose texts from different registers and sampled the text basis in a way that expert writing and user generated content (= UGC) are represented both (60:40%).

Annotation Approach. The definition of termhood is widely divergent across the different gold standards. In Genia and CRAFT, the annotation is very strict, as specific syntactic patterns and semantic contraints are given. Both the work by Bernier-Colborne and Drouin (2014) and the TTC terms have a more liberal annotation scheme, partly following the rules proposed by L'Homme (2004). Bernier-Colborne and Drouin (2014) limit the annotation semantically to items denoting components of cars and for TTC, term candidates were preselected by a term extraction tool. For the ACL RD-TEC gold standards and the BitterCorpus, the definition of termhood is particularly liberal, as termhood is rather loosely defined. They mainly rely on the association an annotator has with respect to a term or to a domain (e.g. by structuring terms in a mindmap) and provide theoretical background about terminology.

For our work, we aim at a compromise between generality of annotation and restriction of outgrowths. Because of the breadth and the stylistic variability of the DIY text basis, we do not set strict

corpora	total	used	corpora	total	used	corpora	total	used
wiki	$4.31 * 10^5$	30,915	FAQs	4,805	347	project	$2.16 * 10^6$	2,701
expert projects	55,430	3,971	encyclopedia	6,059	449	forum	$2.34 * 10^7$	29,293
marketing texts	35,452	2,540	book	54,005	3,868			
tips and tricks	12,711	904	tool manuals	69,831	5,012			

Table 2: Distribution of tokens by subcorpus: expert (two left-most) and user texts (right)

rules for the annotation, e.g. by limiting the syntactic or semantic shape of terms by predefined POS-patterns or predefined ontology elements onto which the terms would have to be mapped. However, we give positive and negative examples, and guiding rules elaborated after extensive discussion about the relation of DIY terms to their domain.

3 Corpus and Domain: from User-Generated to Standard Text

We use a corpus of German texts of the DIY domain, which is thematically about non-professional builds and repairs at home. There are different text sources available, containing texts produced by domain experts as well as by interested lay users. The latter mainly consists of forum posts collected from several online DIY-forums, e.g. from project descriptions or inquiries for instructions. Experts texts include an online encyclopedia and a wiki for DIY work, tools and techniques. The corpus used for the work described here contains ca. 11 M words in total, with 20% expert text vs. 80% user-generated data.

For the manually annotated part, we aim at a balanced extraction of text data from all the different sources. Thematically, we only excluded gardening activities, which we do not see as a part of the DIY domain. The corpus is balanced to include 40% user texts and 60% expert texts. In total, 80,000 tokens are extracted. Since we annotate terms in context (token-based), complete sentences are extracted. We thus sample subcorpora proportionally to their orginal size, to reach a total of 48,000 tokens of expert text plus 32,000 tokens of UGC (see Table 2). All sentences are shuffled.

4 Annotation

4.1 Procedure and Design of Annotations

General Procedure   The annotation guidelines were created in discussion rounds with 6 to 7 participants who have experience in terminology extraction. All are semi-experts of the domain, because they have been dealing with terminology extraction from the DIY domain for more than one year. The guidelines were influenced by terminology theory, peculiarities observed when analysing the text data and practical issues, to ensure a consistent annotation. The actual annotation is being produced by three (of the above) annotators; at the time of writing, two annotators have finished half of the corpus, i.e. 40,000 tokens are annotated.

Annotation Tool   We use **WebAnno** (Yimam et al. (2013), de Castilho et al. (2016)) as an annotation tool, a multi-user tool with a several annotation modes and a visualisation of the annotation. In our case, possible annotations are **spans** (for single- and multiword terms) and **relations** (used here to link separated parts of a term). For the spans, several **values** can be chosen: *domain, domain-zusatz* and *ad-hoc*. While most terms are annotated with *domain*, we use *ad-hoc* for user-coined terms, and *domain-zusatz* (= domain-additional element) for elements that are themselves not terms, but are parts of multiword expressions, e.g. the adverb *freihand* in *freihand sägen*.

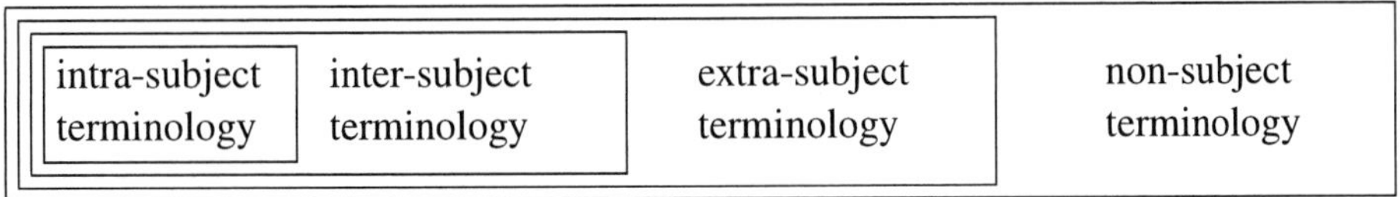

Figure 1: Tiers of terminology (Roelcke (1999)) [our translation]

4.2 Tiers of Terminology and Consequences for the Annotation Approach

The annotation of benchmark sets for terminology is typically implemented as a binary decision. However, it is widely acknowledged that the terminology of a domain is a rather inhomogeneous set. It can be divided into several tiers, e.g. with a distinction between terms which only occur in the very specific vocabulary of a small domain, as opposed to terms which occur with an extended or specialized meaning in one domain but also in other domains or in general language (e.g. Trimble (1985), Beck et al. (2002)). The model by Roelcke (1999) consists of four layers (Figure 1), where the most restrictive one is the **intra-subject terminology** which is specific to the domain. The **inter-subject terminology** is used in the respective domain, but also in others. The **extra-subject terminology** is terminology which does not belong to the domain but is used within it (we call such terms *borrowed terms*). The last group, the **non-subject terminology**, consists of all items used across almost all specific domains. Tutin (2007) calls this 'transdisciplinary vocbulary': it includes the domain-unspecific language of scientific writing (e.g. *evaluation, estimation, observation*) and non-specialized abstract vocabulary (e.g. *to present a problem, to result in*).

Our annotation approach is liberal and our notion of termhood comprises the first three layers of Roelcke's model. As a consequence, often no clear borderline between the DIY domain and other domains can be drawn; following the example of the TaaS project (www.taas-project.eu), we therefore provide the annotation with confidence scores about how many of the annotators agreed on the annotated element to be a term and distinguish between a strict (three annotators agree) and a lenient (two of three annotators agree) annotation.

4.3 Breadth of the Domain: Terminological Richness in the DIY-Domain

The DIY domain is influenced to a high degree by other domains. There is a quite obvious core set of terms which are prototypical (e.g., *drill, fretsaw, circular saw bench, ..*). In addition, there are many terms borrowed from other domains, e.g. from material science or construction techniques. In our annotation, we distinguish between **terminology borrowed from other domains** and **terminology from neighbouring domains**. While texts with intra-subject or inter-subject terms tend to centrally belong to the DIY domain (and describe what we consider to be "typical" DIY activities), borrowing takes place from related domains knowledge about which is necessary for efficient communication in the DIY domain, such as some fields of physics, of material science, construction techniques, etc. We consider fields as neighbouring domains which are carried out professionally, such as sanitary, electrical or heating engineering. Sentences belonging to texts describing work of this kind are disregarded in our annotation.

4.4 Registers: User Language and Jargon

Apart from the broad domain, the wide range of registers is a challenge for annotation. In the user-generated texts, misspellings and user-coined terms (e.g. *Selberbauer, reinhämmern, Filterabrüttlung, mit Hobelmesser "abgemessert"*) have to be addressed. We mark them with the special label *ad-hoc*, to show their terminological relevance but to distinguish them from accepted terms.

The way in which DIY-forum users talk about tools and materials shows their high degree of specialization, even in texts that exhibit signs of conceptual orality (in the sense of Koch and Oesterreicher (1985)). In the 40.0000 words, we identified 71 references of tools in which a highly specialized DIY knowledge is presupposed:

From the standard (expert) text in the domain, we observe that the official denomination of power tools mostly follows a rigid pattern. The names are composed of [BRAND][TYPE][MAIN DESIGNA-TION][SECONDARY DESIGNATION], for example *Metabo Kappsäge KGS 216 M* or *Bosch Tischkreissäge PTS 10 T*. An intuitive way of abbreviating those denominations would be by the type; instead we find highly specific references, close to in-group jargon:

- 16 times the tool was only referenced by its brand name (e.g. *meine Makita, Metabo, ...*);
- 24 times by its main designation (*IXO, PBS, ...*);
- three times by its secondary designation (*0633 ohne Motor, 900er*);
- and 28 times by a combination of main and secondary designation - of different granularity and written in different forms (*GKS 68 BC, PCM8S, ...*).

This special term use increases the number of term types and poses a challenge for automatic term extraction, as well as for coreference resolution in that domain. Furthermore, this way of referencing supports the claim that embedded terms need to be addressed in the manual annotation. Whether a term extraction tool which is sensitive to embedded terms can also identify this kind of references, is still an open question. There are less regular references as well, e.g. abreviations by material (*ODF* instead of *ODF-Platte*), missing size units (*35er Scharnier*), or only sizes are mentioned (*K60-K220* instead of *Schleifpapier der Körnungen K60, K80, .., K220*)). Other special cases are jargon-like abbreviations (*TKS = Tischkreissäge, OF = Oberfräse, HKS = Handkreissäge*).

Another characteristic of user texts is the almost infinite number of domains from where terms can be borrowed: when being creative, everything can be used to do handicrafts with, everything can be (mis)used as a tool or material (*Frühstücksbrett in Fliesenoptik; Geschenkboxen aus Käseschachteln, gedrechselte Kirschen*). Items from these other domains fill areas in DIY which are prototypical, e.g. DIY project names, materials and tools. This makes it harder to decide whether these items are terms. That topics are spread more widely can be shown by the number of sentences annotated in the 40.000 corpus: In the user-generated content (UGC) part, 45.36% of the sentences are annotated, in the expert texts 66.21%. Furthermore, the density of term annotation is higher for the expert texts: in the UGC texts, 9.15% of the tokens are annotated, in the expert texts 17.08%.

4.5 Annotation Approach: Multiword Terms and Term Variants

A special focus of the annotation is on multiword terms (MWTs). We aim to preserve as much of the terminological content in the data as possible. By allowing to annotate discontinuous multiword terms, we enrich the term base.
Besides annotating adjacent MWTs, we also capture MWTs interrupted by terminologically irrelevant material. In *scharfes und gefährliches Messer* (sharp and dangerous knife) *und gefährliches* will not be annotated, while *scharfes Messer* is considered as a term. This annotation is realized by linking together the separate parts of the MWT. A similar case are MWTs which are interrupted by additional terminolog-ical material, e.g. *schwebender (schwibbender) Bogen*, from where two terms can be created by linking: *schwebender Bogen* and *schwibbender Bogen*.
Contrary, e.g. to TTC, we annotate all valid embedded terms. For example, for *freihand gebrochene gerade Kante*, the whole term, *gerade Kante* and *Kante* are annotated.

As we aim at covering all possibly terminologically relevant material, we do not a priori set restric-tions as to the length or POS pattern of term candidates. Anyway, collocational verb-noun pairs (*Holz fräsen, mit Nägeln verbinden*) are not annotated as multiword terms. We aim at distinguishing them from terms. However, this annotation decision leads to an inconsistency at the theoretical level: If the verb-noun pair occurs in its nominalized form (*Nagelverbindung*). As a consequence, we annotate the noun compound form and have this inconsistency; to attenuate this conflict, we also allow idiomatic verb-noun combinations to be annotated. For example in *auf Gehrung sägen, auf Gehrung* is annotated as **domain-zusatz** ('domain additional element') to *sägen*.
Our annotation keeps track of the variety and complexity of syntactic structures in which terms can appear in texts, including non-adjacent parts of multiword expressions.

5 Evaluation

5.1 Inter-Annotator Agreement

Fleiss' kappa (Fleiss et al. (1971)) is used to calculate the inter-annotator agreement. In our annotation, multiword terms, parts of terms and different annotation labels have to be considered. In total, 2514 single-word terms (SWTs) and 511 MWTs are annotated by one annotator, 4269 SWTs and 1353 MWTs by the other one. An item can have multiple labels. Thus, we introduce an IOB format for the terms (term-internal, out-of-domain, beginning of a (multiword) term) and consider the annotation to have 9 labels: IOB * labels *domain, ad-hoc, domain-zusatz.* Fleiss' kappa is calculated for every label and the result is averaged. We achieve an interannotator agreement of 0.81 which is a substantial agreement according to Landis and Koch (1977).

5.2 Error Analysis: Consistent Differences in MWTs Annotation

Despite our strategy to encourage the annotation of MWTs as well as of their embedded terms, we still find consistent differences in this regard. Two kinds of structural inconsistencies are prevalent:

Adj N In 151 out of 455 adjective-noun sequences annotated in total (by either of the annotators), one annotator annotated the whole phrase while the other one annotated only the noun. When analysing the relevant phrases, it is striking that in these cases the adjectives are evaluative (*handliche Fräse*), uninformative (*gängiger Handhobel*), underspecified dimension adjectives (*präziser Schnitt*) or related to the given situation (*vordere Schleifplatte*).

N Prep N In 17 out of 86 cases a noun-preposition-noun phrase is annotated as one stretch by one annotator while the other annotator distinguishes between two single word terms. This set consists of nominalized verb-object pairs (*Schleifen von Kanten*), positional descriptions (*Querlöchern in Holzwerkstoffen*) and purpose constructions (*Sägeblätter für Porenbeton*).

We could refine the guidelines down to individual syntactico-semantic patterns (e.g. positional vs. purpose N Prep N groups), but this would not allow us to take the linguistic creativity of the forum authors into account. Similarly, the vagueness of underspecified dimension adjectives seems rather to be the typical property of the style of our texts. As a consequence, the terms extracted from the forum data can at best be partly organized in ontologies.

6 Conclusion

We presented work towards a benchmark dataset for terminology extraction in the DIY domain. Challenges for annotation are the breadth of the domain and the register variety in our corpus. The corpus is characterized by its heterogeneity, as illustrated by a comparison of expert and user-generated text: User-generated text both has a lower density of terms than expert text (expectably) and jargon-like intra-community terminology. The domain as well as the text characteristics of UGC require specific provisions for the different tiers of terminology they contain (e.g. borrowed terms, neighbouring domains).

Our annotation approach is liberal, yet based on precise guidelines where this is realistic. We pay special attention to the annotation of multiword terms including discontinuous ones. We achieve a substantial inter-annotator agreement for the annotation.

At the time of writing, 40,000 tokens are annotated by two annotators. The dataset will be extended to 80,000 tokens and 3 annotators. We are negotiating the right to publish the annotated dataset.

Future work will include the test of term extraction tools against the dataset, possibly an additional annotation of verb+object pairs, as well as an (automatic) annotation of all sentences with markers for conceptual orality (Koch/Oesterreicher). This may provide more evidence about the relationship between register, style and terminology in forum data.

References

Arcan, M., M. Turchi, S. Tonelli, and P. Buitelaar (2014). Enhancing statistical machine tranlsation with bilingual terminology in a cat environment. In *Proceedings of the 11th Biennial Conference of the Association for Machine Translation in the Americas (AMTA 2014)*, pp. 54–64.

Bada, M., M. Eckert, D. Evans, K. Garcia, K. Shipley, D. Sitnikov, W. A. B. Jr., K. B. Cohen, K. Verspoor, J. A. Blake, and L. E. Hunter (2012). Concept annotation in the CRAFT corpus. *BMC Bioinformatics 13*, 161.

Beck, I. L., M. G. McKeown, and L. Kucan (2002). *Bringing words to life*. New York, NY: The Guilford Press.

Bernier-Colborne, G. and P. Drouin (2014). Creating a test corpus for term extractors through term annotation. *Terminology. International Journal of Theoretical and Applied Issues in Specialized Communication 20*(1), 50–73.

de Castilho, E., . R., Mújdricza-Maydt, S. Yimam, S. Hartmann, I. Gurevych, A. Frank, and C. Biemann (2016). A web-based tool for the integrated annotation of semantic and syntactic structures. In *Proceedings of the LT4DH workshop at COLING 2016*, Osaka, Japan. Association for Computational Linguistics.

Fleiss, J. et al. (1971). Measuring nominal scale agreement among many raters. *Psychological Bulletin 76*(5), 378–382.

Handschuh, S. and B. QasemiZadeh (2014). The acl rd-tec: a dataset for benchmarking terminology extraction and classification in computational linguistics. In *COLING 2014: 4th International Workshop on Computational Terminology*.

Kagueura, K. and B. Umino (1996). Methods of automatic term recognition: A review. *Terminology* (3(2)), 259–289.

Kim, J.-D., T. Ohta, Y. Tateisi, and J. Tsujii (2003). Genia corpus—a semantically annotated corpus for bio-textmining. *Bioinformatics 19*(1), 180–182.

Koch, P. and W. Oesterreicher (1985). Sprache der nähe – sprache der distanz. *Romanistisches Jahrbuch 36*(85), 15–43.

Landis, J. R. and G. G. Koch (1977). The measurement of observer agreement for categorical data. *Biometrics 33*(1).

L'Homme, M.-C. (2004). *La terminologie : principes et techniques*. Les Presses de l'Université de Montréal.

Loginova, E., A. Gojun, H. Blancafort, M. Guégan, T. Gornostay, and U. Heid (2012). Reference lists for the evaluation of term extraction tools. In *Proceedings of the 10th International Congress on Terminology and Knowledge Engineering (TKE)*, Madrid, Spain.

QasemiZadeh, B. and A.-K. Schumann (2016). The acl rd-tec 2.0: A language resource for evaluating term extraction and entity recognition methods. In *LREC*.

Roelcke, T. (1999). *Fachsprachen*. Grundlagen der Germanistik. Erich Schmidt Verlag.

Trimble, L. (1985). *English for Science and Technology: A Discourse Approach*. Cambridge: Cambridge University Press.

Tutin, A. (2007). Traitement sémantique par analyse distributionelle des noms transdisciplinaires des écrits scientifiques. *In Actes de TALN*.

Yimam, S. M., I. Gurevych, R. Eckart de Castilho, and C. Biemann (2013, August). Webanno: A flexible, web-based and visually supported system for distributed annotations. In *Proceedings of the 51st Annual Meeting of the Association for Computational Linguistics: System Demonstrations*, Sofia, Bulgaria, pp. 1–6. Association for Computational Linguistics.

A conceptual ontology in the water domain of knowledge to bridge the lexical semantics of stratified discursive strata

Jean-Louis Janin, PhD student, U. Bordeaux Montaigne (`turennejlj@orange.fr`)
Henri Portine, Professor emeritus (`henri.portine@u-bordeaux-montaigne.fr`)

September 2017

Abstract

This paper illustrates the semantic articulation between pivot and satellite lexical units of different discursive strata in the water lexicon model supported by the French Water Academy (*Lexeau* project of a *Bilingual lexicon of water related texts and data*, to improve public awareness of water related issues and ensure a better inter-comprehension among stakeholders. The lexical treatment of the discursive unit "*water withdrawal*" into stratified entries shows the capacity of a domain ontology to set a bridge between discursive strata in different languages, making easier internal and external translations between stakeholders. With more than a hundred lexical entries tested, there is an opportunity for a consortium of realization and a project of a pilot internet application.

1 Introduction

This paper presents one aspect of the lexicon project launched by the French Water Academy to improve public awareness of water related issues and ensure a better inter-comprehension among professional and non professional stakeholders of the domain. The focus is put on the role of the ontology in articulating pivot and satellite stratified lexicon units entered in different discursive strata.

It has been recognized that the meaning of a discursive unit may vary in the domain of water discourse, depending on the audience (Payen (2013)). It may lead to ambiguities and misunderstanding if some words and expressions are received by the audience in a sense which was not foreseen by the speaker or the author, *i.e.* out of the acception he is used to employ and trying to convey in his own discursive stratum. According to the large part of legal and administrative texts in the water domain and the large number of scientists and engineers involved in research and development activities, including humanities, we have introduced two different *technico-scientific (TS)* and *technico-administrative (TA)* discursive strata, together with the *current (C)* discursive stratum, for daily exchanges and media production on water actuality. In everyday life, words are linked to casual and colloquial notions or concepts. We have also introduced a *decisional/incitative (DI)* discursive stratum to take into account other textual productions of the domain. One example is the UN General Assembly Resolution of 2010/07/28 on "The human right to water and sanitation", still to be enforced by normative laws in each member state. The two main features of the stratified lexicon are the one-to-one relationship between conceptual units and pivot lexical units and the ordering of the discursive strata to limit the articulation of pivot units with satellite units of a higher range. The strata are listed with their prefixed label and corpus summary:

- 1-TS Technico-scientific (scientific papers, articles and books);

- 2-DI Decisional incitative (political and legal incitative proposals and decisions);

- 3-TA Technico-administrative (laws, directives, regulation, judicial activity);

- 4-C Current (current exchanges and daily media : press, radio and television.)

This order corresponds to the intuitive idea that concepts of scientific origin are likely to be transferred in the lexicon as pivot lexical units, defined through object and data properties of the ontology and articulated with satellite units in discursive strata of a higher range. An articulation with discursive strata of a lower range would invalidate our assumption, but we could not find any example of it.

After presenting a partition of the water related domain of knowledge, we will present the *model of water movements and anthropic water flows* introduced in the ontology, and one example of a pivot unit articulated with three satellite units. The following discussion focuses on the central place of the ontology in the model device including the end-user. The question of proper names is discussed, together with the relations of our research work in linguistics to lexical semantics and terminology.

2   A partition of the water related domain of knowledge

The water related domain of knowledge has been divided into three parts. The first part, called ONTOLOGY, is an ontology of the concepts, mainly scientific and administrative, structuring human knowledge and activities in water use and aquatic environment conservation and restoration. The output of this part of knowledge is composed of conceptual units, documents and typed individuals (fig. 1).

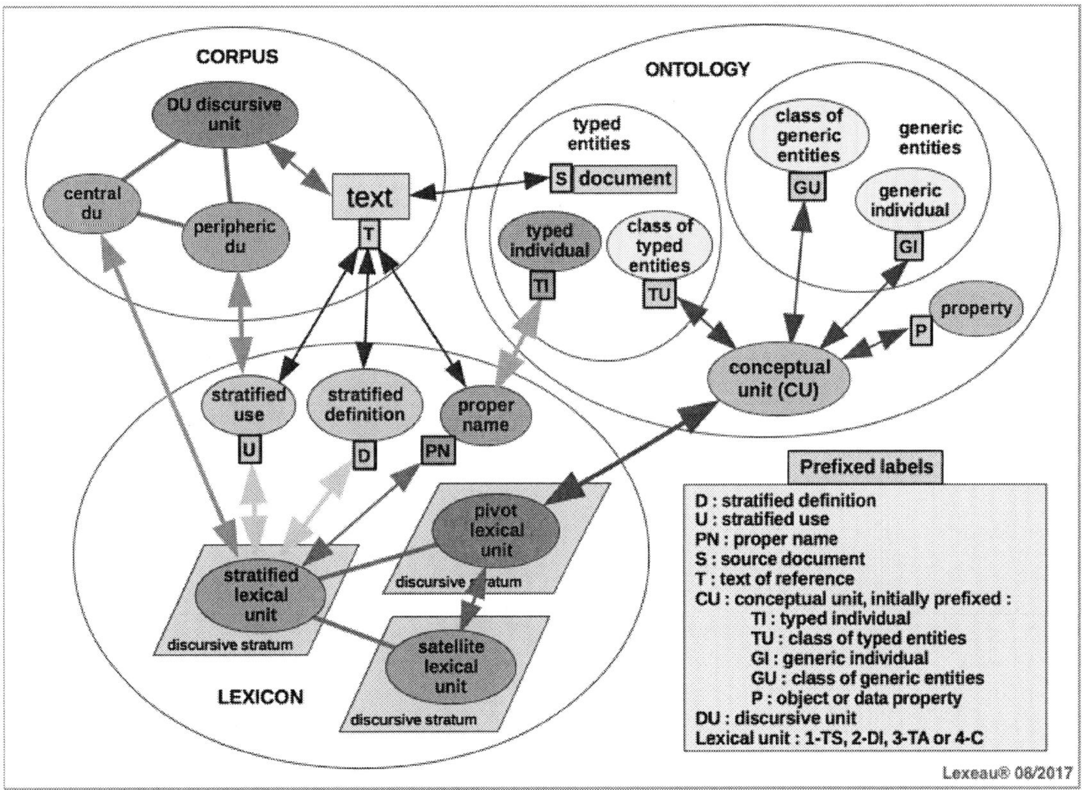

Figure 1:   A partition of the water related domain of knowledge

The second part, called *LEXICON*, is composed of proper names and stratified lexical units. Pivot units have a *one-to-one* relationship with conceptual units and a *one-to-n* relationship with satellite units. The third part of the domain, called *CORPUS*, is composed of recurrent discursive units found in texts referenced in proper names implementation, lexical definitions and stratified examples of use of some lexicon entries. The relevance of the use of concepts — including scientific concepts, except the concepts of mathematics, physics and chemistry — is textual: hydrology, geology and so on are stated in texts. That is why corpus linguistics is of overall importance for ontologies. The central discursive units are linked with the lexical units and the peripheric ones are linked with the stratified examples of use.

3 A conceptual model of water movements and anthropic water flows

The water withdrawals are modeled as upstream water movements generating anthropic flows recovered by downstream water movements. The graph of the model is presented fig. 2. We have added, on a yellow background, the labels of the class relations (*object relations*) and, on an orange one, the labels of a set of related individuals : The *Water withdrawal1* generates the *Water flow (anthropic)1* which is recovered by the *Water restitution1*. The figure 3 presents the creation of the three conceptual units,

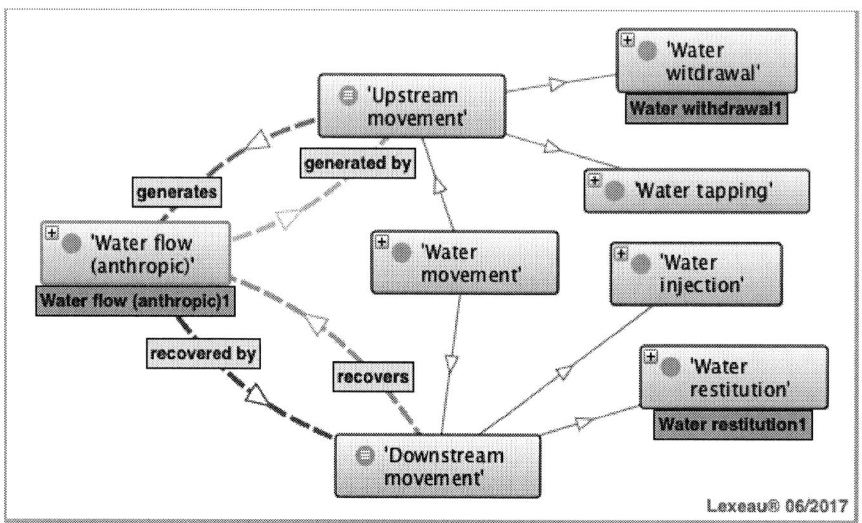

Figure 2: The model of water movements and anthropic flows with a set of related individuals

prefixed CU, after creating the three concepts, prefixed TU, as individuals in their original labelled class, further added to the class *Conceptual unit* as individuals of the hyper-class *Typed entity*. To present the

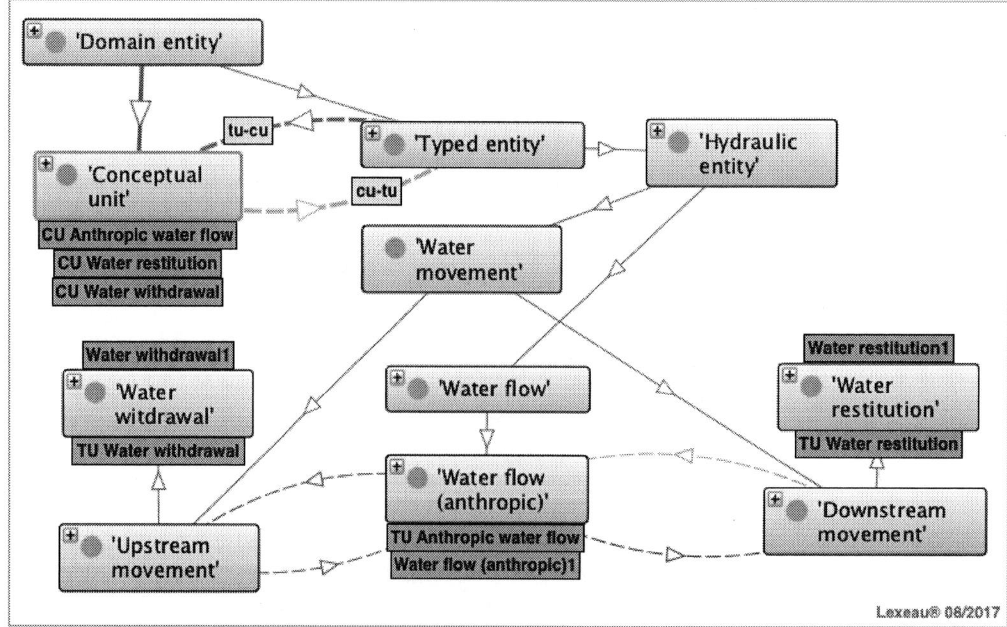

Figure 3: Generating three conceptual units through individuals created in labelled classes

lexicalisation process and text-based processes within and between the three parts of figure 1, we have used the same software (Protege 5.2) to edit a *project ontology* of all the entities of the partition.

4 Articulating pivot and satellite lexical units

A graph of the *Conceptual unit* and *Stratified lexical unit* related classes and of the four sub-classes of lexical units is presented figure 4, with the pivot-satellite articulations between these units. The four related labelled lexicon units and their labelled relations have been added on orange and rosy backgrounds.

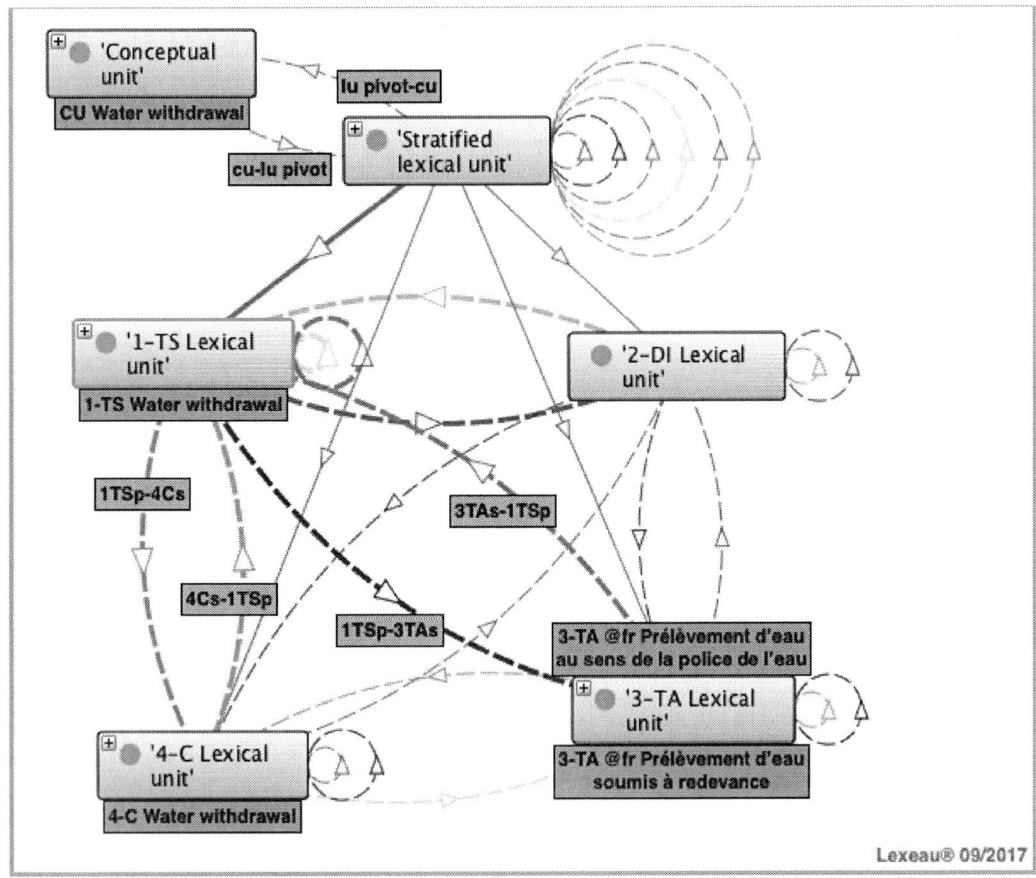

Figure 4: An example of one pivot lexical unit articulated with three satellite units

The definitions of the pivot units are derived from the object and data properties of the ontology entities whose labels are saved as concepts and further lexicalised (cf. fig. 2 and 3), leading to :

- D 1-TS Water withdrawal : *A water extraction carried out by an operator in a water body which generates an intermittent or permanent water flow. The operation can be associated with an extraction water work equipped with a volumetric meter*

- D 1-TS Anthropic water flow : *Water flow permanent or intermittent over a given period, in a water use concern wih a physical or legal person. With a total volume and a maximum flow rate measured or estimated, it is associated with an upstream water movement (water withdrawal in a water body or water tapping in a water network) and a downstream water movement (water restitution in a water body or water injection in a water network)*

The construction of the lexicon is based on the articulations of pivot lexical units with satellite units, looking for other acceptions of the same word or a closely related form in a different discursive stratum. An example is presented figure 4 with the pivot unit *1-TS Water withdrawal* and the satellite units *4-C Water withdrawal*. Two entries of *water withdrawal* are found in the French administrative discourse, with two different meanings referring to the "police de l'eau" and "redevances de l'agence de l'eau" national practices with no exact equivalent in Great Britain, at least to our knowledge. The entries are defined in French and just labelled with the "@fr" prefix in the *Anglo-british* version. (fig. 5 and 6).

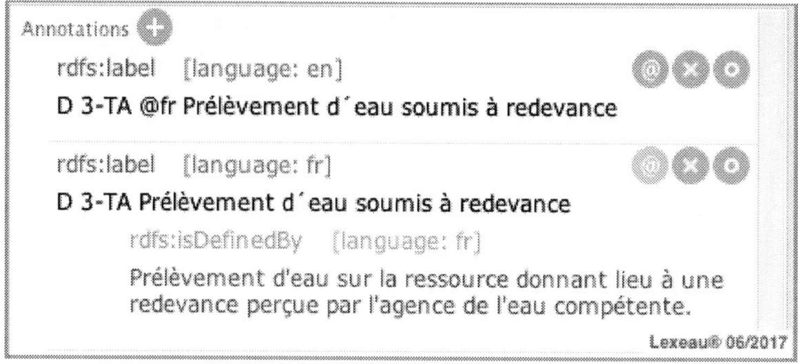

Figure 5: "3-TA Water withdrawal" first acception in France

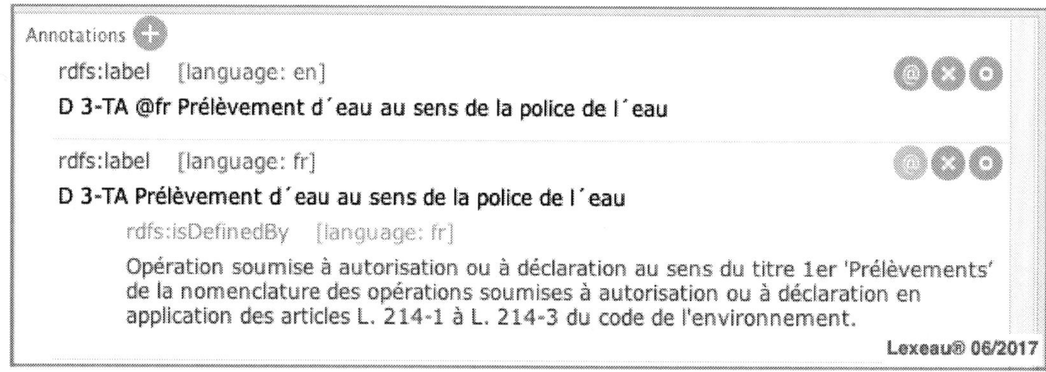

Figure 6: "3-TA Water withdrawal" second acception in France

To finalize the English version, possible administrative acceptions of *Water withdrawal* should be checked in the United States, Canada, Australia, New Zealand and other English speaking countries.

Looking for a satellite lexical unit in a current bilingual discourse, we have found it in a plural form, on the OECD Data site on water withdrawals, with a bilingual definition (fig. 7).

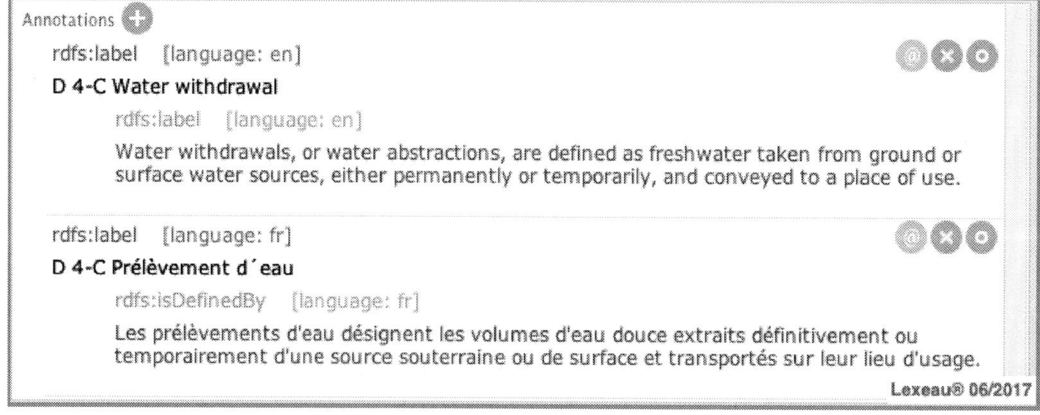

Figure 7: A bilingual OECD definition of "4-C Water withdrawal"

The lexical unit *4-C Water withdrawal* is defined as a volume of water withdrawn yearly for human use, except for hydroelectricity production. It is expressed in millions of cubic meters per country on the tables and maps of the OECD site. This meaning is easier to understand than considering the *hydraulic operation* modeled in the ontology, with its related entities, or the *administrative operation* authorized by the French *police de l'eau* or taxed by the French *Agence de l'eau* under specific circumstances.

With two different acceptions, the French administration as a whole is not prepared to match individual data collected by the "police de l'eau" and the "Agence de l'eau" (operator, volume of water withdrawn, final user, etc.) as the practice on both sides do not state how these data on water withdrawals should match in the *real world*. One way to overcome these difficulties would be to get more information on both sides, typically about the downstream operation on the flow of the water withdrawn, separating the notions of water movement and water flow, as proposed in the definitions of *1-TS Water withdrawal* and *1-TS Anthropic water flow*, in a scientific approach of the hydraulic concepts involved.

5   Discussion

5.1   A conceptual ontology at the heart of the project

Bringing a conceptual ontology within the construction process of the water lexicon raises the question of its feasibility and its maintenance among a community of contributors, mainly scientists, engineers and jurists, in such a vast domain of knowledge. The main issue of the project is to find out, in public and private enterprises, trained contributors to update the ontology on the long term in agreement with their employer. Existing ontologies or relational data bases have already been developed successfully for specific uses in the industry of water services or scientific laboratories, with specific concepts and terms involved in their internal use. The aim of the project is by no mean to plunder existing software or replace it by a new one. In the modeling of water movements, the objective was to organize existing and new concepts and label them on this particular theme so they could be shared and traced in published texts, in English and/or in French, and further introduced as lexicon entries. With no direct users, the ontology may contribute to share the labels of scientific entities and facilitate inter-comprehension between scientists and engineers, and further institutional data exchanges. The place of the ontology in the device model is presented in figure 8. Another issue is the sharing of concepts with energy and food

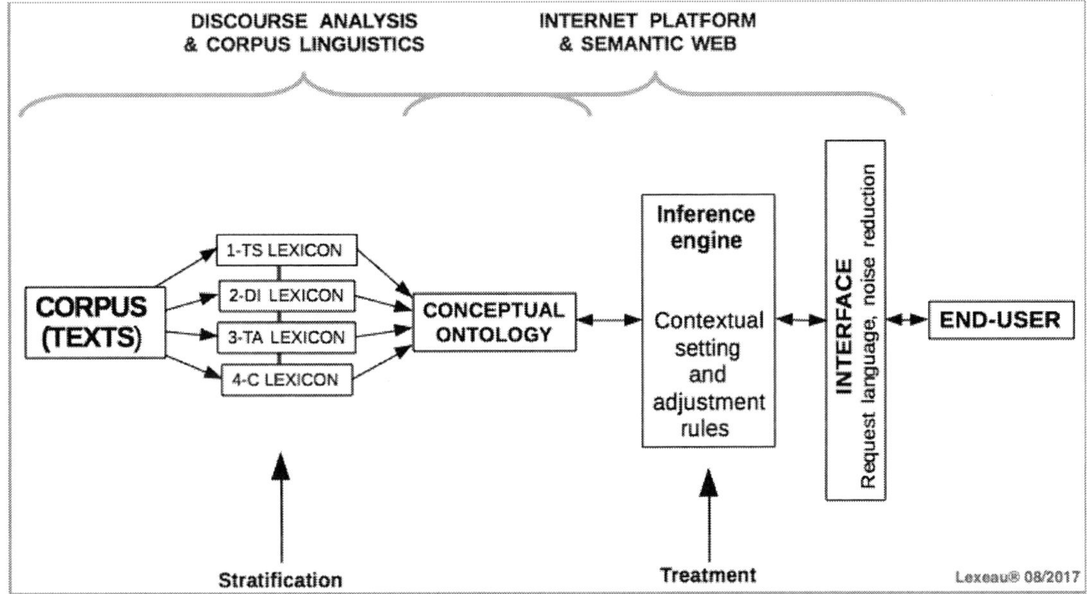

Figure 8: An overall model of the device

related knowledge domains. This issue is addressed with the notion of energy, water and food *security nexus* pointed out by Bazilian et al. (2011) and updated by Howarth and Monasterolo (2016). It should take place through the study of an ontology alignement in the common domain of knowledge and activity.

5.2   The question of proper names

Proper names — as proper nouns, including acronyms, and nominal phrases — are of considerable importance in the domain of water. They are used to name places, persons, documents, events, etc. We follow the position of Saul Kripke on the nature of proper names as rigid designators, against the descriptivist theory of Russell and Frege, assuming their identity as a collection of finite descriptions (Kripke (1982), Kripke (1980)). In our project, nevertheless, proper names are issued from the individuals of the typed classes of the domain entities. The class object property and data property assertions of these individuals correspond, when they are phrased, to the finite descriptions of the descriptive theory. The proper names introduced in the lexicon are not stratified, with no use to define them as it would duplicate the properties of their homologue individual in the ontology.

5.3   The relation to lexical semantics

Our relation to lexical semantics in the project follows the historical evolution of the discipline. At the start, lexicology tried to assess the sense of words, considered as isolated entities, within a network of synonyms and antonyms (cf. Cadiot and Habert (1997), Panier and Rémi-Giraud (2003), Victorri and Fuchs (1996)). Further relations appeared later : hyperonymy *vs* hyponymy, then meronymy, and the question of holonymy. The research focus moved then on cooccurrences and collocations, leaving the domain of the auto centered lexicon for a corpus-based lexicon driven by discursive activities. Our research work takes into account the discourse and the social activity where it takes place (small talk, commercial, administrative, educational, scientific), which raises the question of our connection with sociolinguistics, when we infer a stratified lexicon, depending on the audience (cf. Labov (1972), on speech style).

In its bilingual aspect, our work is in debt with English textbooks (Murphy (2010), Cruse (1986)), including a grammar (Huddleston (1988)). Handbooks did help to get some insight on the processing of language by computers and knowledge-based systems (Mitkov (2003), Baader et al. (2007) and we are concerned with recent developments on *Big Data* (Bidoit and Doucet (2017)). Our work is confronted and in debt with classical linguistic results about conceptual analysis (Wierzbicka (1985)), sense-text linguistics (Mel'čuk and Polguère (2007)), the generative lexicon (Pustejovsky (1995)) and *inferential* lexical semantics (Kayser (1997a), Kayser (1997b)), as proposed in the abstract of the last reference [1] :

> Actually, what matters [in lexical semantics] are the inferences which are warranted by the use of a word in a context; the existence of a referent in some universe of discourse is merely a possible by-product of these inferences.

The discursive affiliation of a lexicon entry depends on the professional affiliation of the speaker and the inferences that he can make and share with his audience. This leads to different acceptions of the same word and implies different combinations with other words in the text. The journalist having in mind a *water withdrawal* as a volume of water withdrawn in one year will not make any distinction between this water withdrawal and the corresponding yearly *water flow*. He would not understand what *water restitution* stands for, without a clear view of the model presented here. Same thing for the administrative authority licensing a given operator for a given water withdrawal, with no clear distinction between the operator and the end user and no information on the stage of use (final *vs* not final) and the level of use (collective *vs* private) of the water withdrawn.

---

[1] `http://www.persee.fr/doc/lfr_0023-8368_1997_num_113_1_5372`

The use of current expressions may result in considerable ambiguities and erroneous conclusions. As pointed out by G. Payen [Payen (2013) p.113], the current discourse does not always make the difference between a problem of a *water shortage* due to the lack of water resource and a situation of *water shortage* in an urban district out of reach of the municipal drinking water network of the town.

5.4   The relation to terminology

Terminology is above all technical and scientific. It has little interest in social relations. It is a normative activity, to facilitate the integration in a native language of words and expressions already used in a foreign second langage, most of them in English, with a highly controlled definition in the source language. The terminologist tries to accommodate the original definition in his native language. To fulfill business and trade issues, the activity is *prescriptive*, looking for a one-to-one relation between the terms of each language to facilitate the translation of documents. Linguists dealing with terminology are well aware of the difficulties of their task (Depecker (2003), Condamines (2016)).

We are engaged in a *descriptive* corpus sourced activity, in French and in English, with no prescriptive pretension and the clear notion that conceptual units may not have their equivalent in two langages, which can be rendered in the bilingual ontology and the lexicon entries. The tools used to scrutinize the thematic corpora of the project for recurrent discursive units will be able to analyse the use of prescribed terms in a given context, therefore contributing to some terminological activity.

6   Conclusion

After presenting the ontology of the Lexeau project in previous papers (Janin and Portine (2016) and Janin (2016)), this paper has presented, through the example of a model of water movements and anthropic water flows, the role of a conceptual ontology in the water related domain of knowledge and the sense of its threefold partition. In our example, the class object and data properties of the ontology are used to create stable definitions, in the technico-scientific discursive stratum, of the pivot lexical units *1-TS Water withdrawal* and *1-TS Anthropic water flow*. It allows to create other lexicon entries as satellite units to the pivot units, such as *4-C Water withdrawal*, in the current discursive stratum. An overall model of the device with its different modules has been presented. The treatment of proper names has been discussed, together with the relations of our research work to lexical semantics and terminology.

Intellectual activities are not limited to research activities, describing scientific phenomena. They have their place in professional activities of the water domain, aiming at a sound technical, commercial, ecological and legal water management. They have also their place in daily activities, in current exchanges and in the media production on water use, water pollution and security matters (drought and floods). These activities share the same words in different meanings, defined in different discursive strata. Through the example of *water withdrawal*, we have shown that the lexical units in the administrative and current discourse are underspecified in terms of the *real world objects* and *persons*. Their articulation with a pivot lexical unit with complete specifications is crucial for a better understanding of the stakeholders of water uses and withdrawals. The solution of internal *translation* difficulties in one language applies also when dealing with two languages, with legal and political impacts in international affairs.

With more than a hundred discursive units tested on the model device, the construction of an ontology combined with textual investigations appears to be a sound way of bridging current and specialized discourses and a promising contribution to mutual inter-comprehension of stake holders in the water domain. There is now an opportunity to shape a consortium of realization of a pilot project (an internet application). The goal would be to develop and test the application on thematic priorities, with minimal development expenses and the help of professional contributors and non professional end users.

References

Baader, F., D. Calvanese, D. L. McGuiness, D. Nardi, and P.-S. P. F. (2007). *The Descritption Logic Handbook*. Cambridge: Cambridge University Press.

Bazilian, M., R. Holger, M. Howells, S. Hermann, D. Arent, D. Gielen, P. Steduto, A. Mueller, P. Komor, R. S. Tol, and K. K. Yumkella (2011). Considering the energy, water and food nexus: Towards an integrated modelling approach. *Energy Policy (Elsevier) 39*, 7896–7906.

Bidoit, N. and A. Doucet (2017). *Les Big Data à découvert*, Chapter La diversité des données, pp. 24–25. Paris: CNRS éditions.

Cadiot, P. and B. Habert (1997). *Aux sources de la polysémie nominale*. Larousse.

Condamines, A. (2016). Vers la définition de nouvelles langues contrôlées pour limiter le "risque langagier". In LIMSI (Ed.), *Atelier risques et TAL (JEP-TALN- RECITAL 2016)*, Paris.

Cruse, D. (1986). *Lexical semantics*. Cambridge: Cambridge University Press.

Depecker, L. (2003). *Entre signe et concept, éléments de terminologie générale*. Presse Sorbonne Nouvelle.

Howarth, C. and I. Monasterolo (2016). Understanding barriers to decision making in the UK energy-food-water nexus: The added value of interdisciplinary approaches. *Environmental Science and Policy (Elsevier) 61*, 53–60.

Huddleston, R. (1988). *English grammar : an outline*. Cambridge: Cambridge University Press.

Janin, J.-L. (2016). Sélection et typage des acronymes de PREVIRISQ INONDATIONS 2016. In AFEPTB (Ed.), *Les Ateliers PREVIRISQ INONDATIONS - 17 octobre 2016 - Centre des Congrès de Lyon*.

Janin, J.-L. and H. Portine (2016). L'ontologie du projet lexeau®. In Université de Bordeaux (Ed.), *Actes JFO 2016 (ISBN 978-2-9558601-0-6)*.

Kayser, D. (1997a). *La représentation des connaissances*. Paris: Hermès.

Kayser, D. (1997b). La sémantique lexicale est d'abord inférentielle. *Langue française Aux sources de la polysémie nominale*(113), 92–106.

Kripke, S. (1980). *Naming and necessity*. Cambridge (Mass.): Harvard Unuversity Press.

Kripke, S. (1982). *La logique des noms propres*. Les éditions de minuit (Naming and necessity).

Labov, W. (1972). *Sociolinguistics*, Chapter The Study of Language in its Social Context, pp. 180–202. Penguin Books.

Mel'čuk, I. and A. Polguère (2007). *Lexique actif du français*. Bruxelles: De Boeck.

Mitkov, R. (2003). *The Oxford hanbook of computational linguistics*. Oxford: Oxford University Press.

Murphy, M. L. (2010). *Lexical meaning*. Cambridge: Cambridge University Press.

Panier, L. and S. Rémi-Giraud (2003). *La polysémie ou l'empire des sens : lexique, discours, représentations*. Lyon: Presses universitaires de Lyon.

Payen, G. (2013). *De l'eau pour tous ! Abandonner les idées reçues, affronter les réalités*. Paris: Armand Colin.

Pustejovsky, J. (1995). *The generative lexicon*. Cambridge (Mass.): MIT Press.

Victorri, B. and C. Fuchs (1996). *La polysémie : Construction dynamique du sens*. Paris: Hermès.

Wierzbicka, A. (1985). *Lexicography and conceptual analysis*. Ann Arbor: Karoma.

GeoDict: an integrated gazetteer

Jacques Fize
UMR TETIS, CIRAD
Montpellier, France
`jacques.fize@cirad.fr`

Gaurav Shrivastava
Birla Institute of Science and Technology
Pilani, India
`gauravsh033@gmail.com`

Abstract

Nowadays, spatial analysis in text is widely considered as important for both researchers and users. In certain fields such as epidemiology, the extraction of spatial information in text is crucial and both resources and methods are necessary. In most of spatial analysis process, gazetteer is a commonly used resource. A gazetteer is a data source where toponyms (place name) are associated with concepts and their geographic footprint. Unfortunately, most of publicly available gazetteer are incomplete due to their initial purpose. Hence, we propose Geodict, an integrated gazetteer that contains basic yet precise information (multilingual labels, administrative boundaries polygon, etc.) which can be customized. We show its utility when using it for geoparsing (extraction of spatial entities in text). Early evaluation on toponym resolution shows promising results.

1 Introduction

Nowadays, spatial analysis in text is widely considered as important for both researchers and users. For example, Google search engine is used 30 to 40%[1] of the time for spatial queries such as: *pizzeria in Pao Alto* or *Hotel near Coutances*, etc. In certain fields of research such as epidemiology, extracting information in text is crucial. In epidemiology, textual data represent 60% of the available information (Barboza, 2014). In particular, to study an epidemic spreading, different methods and techniques are necessary to extract spatial information in text.

Most of spatial analysis process are depending on geographical datasets such as gazetteers. A gazetteer is data source where toponyms (place names) are linked to concepts and their geographic footprint (Hill, 2000) (See Figure 1).

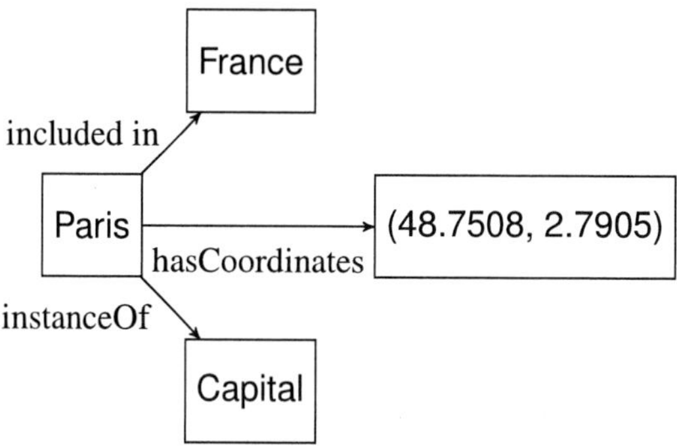

Figure 1: Example of information linked to Paris in a gazetteer

---

[1]Google Pinpoint 2012, London: `https://www.youtube.com/watch?v=ucYiMBfyNfo`

The extraction of spatial entities or *geoparsing* can be considered as one of the most important part in spatial analysis. Geoparsing is generally a two steps process:

(i) **Toponym identification**, *e.g. There is town near our house called <u>Paris</u>*

(ii) **Toponym resolution**, *e.g. Paris ⇔ Paris, France? Paris, Missouri? Paris, Illinois? ...*

Geoparsing is also known to be difficult due to text characteristics such as: context, language and text size. We can mention works on short text such as tweet or SMS for which the task is particularly challenging (Li and Sun, 2014; Zenasni et al., 2016).

Until now, most of publicly available gazetteers are incomplete because of their original usage. For example, Getty is destined to be used to catalog work of art. Thus complete data on administrative boundaries or precise coordinates are unnecessary. However, other users may have different usages and create new gazetteers by adding or restraining information to their needs. In this paper, we present Geodict, a customizable gazetteer that contains basic yet precise information (multilingual labels, administrative boundaries polygon, etc.) and its usage in geoparsing. Geodict is available **here**[2].

This paper is organized as follows. In Section 2, we review commonly used gazetteers and geoparsing methods. In Section 3, we present Geodict, its creation process and the associated features we defined for. Then in Section 4, a geoparsing use-case process using Geodict is presented. Finally, we conclude in Section 5.

2 Related Works

This section outlines related works on gazetteers and geoparsing.

2.1 Gazetteers

Geonames Geonames is a publicly available gazetteer. It contains more than 8 million entries linked to different information such as: *a unique ID, coordinates, used name, aliases, etc.* Each entry is classified by a tuple (class, code) *e.g (P, PPL) → Populated Place.*

Getty The Getty gazetteer or TGN (The Getty Thesaurus of Geographic Names) is part of datasets (AAT[3], ULAN[4]) used to improve the access of information about art, architecture and material culture. It is composed of approximately 1.3 million entries. Since Getty is destined for arts cataloging, data such as coordinates are less precise and not aimed for GIS[5] (Geographic Information System). Interestingly, each entry has its label in different languages and sometimes the time period when it is used. Compared to Geonames, each entry may have coordinates of their administrative boundaries. However, the boundaries are only described by two points.

Others geographical resources like Geodict propose datasets built on linked open datasets. (Stadler et al., 2012) propose LinkedGeoData, a translation of OpenStreetMap to RDF model. However, it's hasn't been updated since 2015.

2.2 Geoparsing

Most of methods with good accuracy are rule-based. (Li et al., 2003; DeLozier et al., 2015) and (Clough et al., 2004) define a special gazetteer where each spatial entity is associated with a unique toponym based on different criteria (popularity, size, population, etc.). (Lieberman et al., 2010; Rauch et al., 2003;

---

[2] http://dx.doi.org/10.18167/DVN1/MWQQOQ
[3] The Art & Architecture Thesaurus
[4] Union List of Artist Names
[5] http://www.getty.edu/research/tools/vocabularies/tgn/about.html

Gazetteer	Nb. of SE[1]	A.B.[2]	Linked to	Customizable
Getty	1477816	✔[3]		
Geonames	11301264			
Geodict	4130301	✔	Geonames, OSM, Wikidata, Wikipedia	✔

[1] Spatial Entities
[2] Administrative Boundaries
[3] Two coordinates (rectangle boundaries)

Table 1: Comparison with other gazetteers

Li et al., 2003) or CLAVIN[6] use geographical scope defined by fixed spatial entities to disambiguate spatial entities. (Rauch et al., 2003; Clough et al., 2004) propose to use contextual information contained in words preceding (resp. following) a toponym.

Data-driven techniques adopt machine learning methods to disambiguate toponyms (Grossman and Frieder, 2004). The main issue of this method dwells within its training corpus which is not available in the community.

(Overell and Rger, 2008) propose to use co-occurrence models. Each document is associated with a list of words ordered by co-occurrences. Then, association rules can be extracted such as *Paris* → *France*.

3 GeoDict

A large number of geographical datasets and gazetteers store different pieces of information. Recently, data description strategies were harmonized. Hence datasets are strongly linked and follow similar representation formats (RDF model), it eases data aggregation from different datasets. To build Geodict, we chose to collect detailed representation for each attribute using different sources: Wikidata, Geonames, OpenStreetMap. Thanks to the policy within the Semantic Web (Berners-Lee et al., 2001), all mentioned data sources are easy to link. Ultimately, each entry in Geodict is associated with the attributes described in Table 2.

Wikidata. Wikidata is a publicly available and editable knowledge base. Entries in Wikidata are distinguished in two types: (i) items that represent all *things* in human knowledge *e.g. queen, Barack Obama, etc.*, (ii) properties that allow to represent information of items. Each item is described through *statements* which are composed of:

- a property, *e.g. country (P47)*

- one or multiple value(s), *e.g. France (Q142)*

- information reference/source, *e.g. https://en.wikipedia.org/wiki/Paris*

OpenStreetMaps. OpenStreetMap is free and editable map of the whole world. It was created to help people to access geographical data. OSM entries are divided in three types: *node, way, relation*. Each element is described with one or multiple *tags*. For example, Paris could be associated with tags like: *name=Paris; wikidata=Q90; alt_name=Lutèce.*

---

[6] https://clavin.bericotechnologies.com/about-clavin/
[7] P47: Share border with *e.g. France shares border with Belgium*
[8] P131: located in the administrative territorial entity *e.g. Paris is located in the adm. terr. entity Ile de France*
[9] P706: located on terrain feature *e.g. The Liberty Statue is located on terrain feature "Liberty Island"*

Field	Source	Example Value
Unique ID	Wikidata	*Q30: USA*
Labels	Wikidata	*fr: Cologne, de: Köln, etc.*
Administrative Boundaries	OpenStreetMap	*[[0,1],[1,0], …]*
Coordinates	Wikidata	*(48.7508,2.7905)*
Class(es)/Concept(s)	Geonames	*(P, PPL): populated place*
Spatial relationships (P47[7], P131[8], P706[9])	Wikidata	*See footnotes*

Table 2: Entry associated information

	Frequency
A (country, region, …)	281951
P (city, village,…)	856962
R (road, railroad, …)	292124
S (spot, building, farm, …)	642148
T (mountain, hill, rock, …)	1014332
U (undersea)	4317
V (forest, health, …)	10130
H (stream, lake, …)	976335
L (parks, area, …)	56943
With boundaries	172 645
Total	4 130 301

Table 3: Statistics on Geodict

3.1 Gazetteer creation

The creation process of Geodict is composed of 5 steps:

1. **Harvest basic information on Wikidata** (labels, coordinates, etc.). Since Wikidata is a general knowledge base, we only keep entries which one of the two following conditions:

   - Has a Geonames ID or a OpenStreetMapID (*resp. P1566* and *P402*)
   - Or has the property P706 or P131

2. **Associate one or multiple class(es) (city, canyon, etc.) for each entry**. We associate each available value contained in the property P31[10] (*e.g populated places*) to a Geonames class-code tuple (*e.g P, PPL*).

3. **Find the missing links**. All these data sources are strongly linked. However some links are missing and especially in OpenStreetMap entries. More precisely, some of the entries in OpenStreetMap don't have a Wikidata link but only a Wikipedia link. Fortunately, we know that each Wikipedia page is linked to a Wikidata entry (Vrandečić and Krötzsch, 2014) and each of these links are stored in Wikidata. Thus we search the missing links in OpenStreetMap entries by searching their Wikipedia link in Wikidata.

4. **Add user defined properties.** We associate user specified properties in Wikidata with each entity.

5. **Add the administrative boundaries.** Polygon coordinates representing administrative boundary(ies) are associated with their corresponding entry in the gazetteer.

Once the whole process is executed, a resulting gazetteer is created with 4,130,301 spatial entities divided in different Geonames class as illustrated in Table 3.

---

[10]P31: instance of *e.g. Barack Obama is an instance of [person, president, lawyer, etc.]*

3.2 Comparison with other gazetteers

We compare Geodict to other available gazetteers using three characteristics: (i) the number of spatial entities, (ii) linked datasets, (iii) if boundaries are available and (iv) if it is customizable. Table 1 sums up the characteristics for all gazetteers.

Obviously, Geodict isn't the most exhaustive because of specific constraints and the chosen pivot dataset (Wikidata). For example, by comparing Geodict with Geonames, we have less entries ($\approx$36% of Geonames). However, we remind that each spatial entity in Geodict is associated with complete information necessary to the geoparsing process. In order to fit different purposes, Geodict is customizable and linked to commonly used dataset such as Wikipedia. Future work will concentrate on different extraction processes to increase Geodict coverage.

3.3 Featured methods

To exploit the data in Geodict, basic methods were implement for spatial analysis.

Data access. We choose to store Geodict in an Elasticsearch (ES) instance for two reasons. First, running queries on Elasticsearch is really efficient. Second, ES is associated with various data types (nested object, geo-shape) and their related queries.

We implement simple functions such as:

- *ExistsInGazeteer*(toponym)

- *getEntityWithWikidataID*(WikiID)

- *getEntitiesWithLabel*(label,[lang])

Recently, the scientific community has taken an interest in spatial reasoning using GeoSPARQL with triple store (Anelli et al., 2016). Hence, we plan to propose Geodict using Linked Data suggested formats (JSON-LD, N-TRIPLES, etc.).

Adjacency Test. In order to detect two adjacent spatial entities, we use three methods:

- Using the separating axis theorem (SAT) on administrative boundaries convex hulls.

- Use Wikidata P47 (share borders with) properties.

- Use P131 (located in administrative territorial entity) and P706 (located on terrain feature). Two objects are considered adjacent if they belong to a common value inside those properties. For example, the Statue of Liberty and the Governors Island are adjacent since both of their P131 value are equal to Manhattan.

Customization Depending on different applications, users may need complimentary data. Since Wikidata is a general knowledge base, users are allowed to indicate relevant and complimentary properties to extract. However, Wikidata stored information can be incomplete. Fortunately, Geodict is stored in JSON format and stored entries are linked to common database such as Wikipedia. Thus, complementary information from other data sources can be easily merged with Geodict.

The source code of Geodict is available at `https://bitbucket.org/thedark10rd/geodict`.

4 A case study: using Geodict for geoparsing

In the previous section, we introduced Geodict, a gazetteer with basic yet precise information and customizable. In the following section, we present a usecase for geoparsing using Geodict.

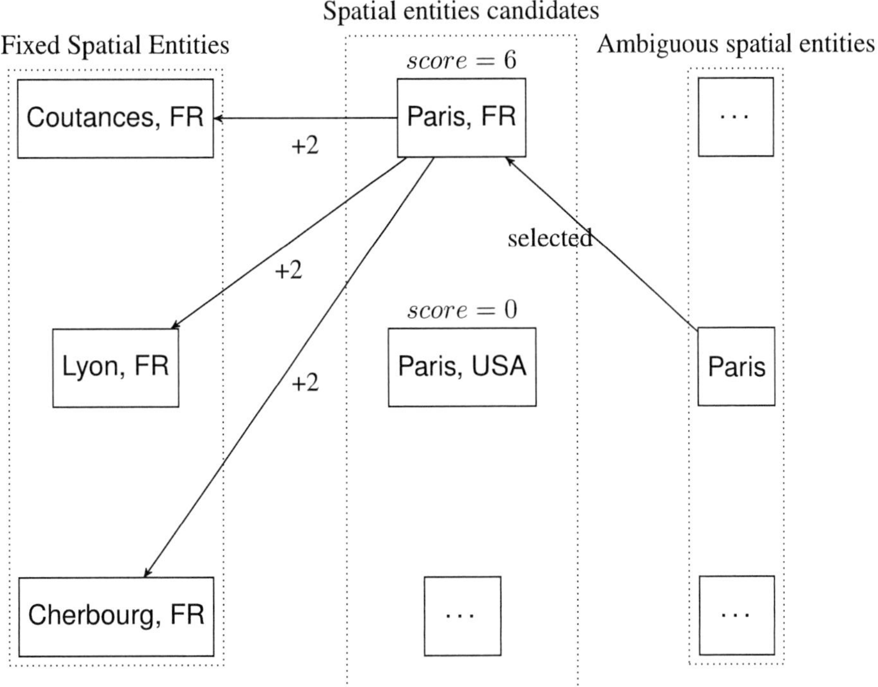

Figure 2: Example of toponym resolution with *Paris*

4.1 Toponym identification

To identify toponyms, we use a NER or Named Entity Recognizer. Various NERs have been proposed such as *StanfordNER* (Finkel et al., 2005), *NLTK*[11] and *Polyglot* (Al-Rfou et al., 2015). Since it supports 40 languages, we chose Polyglot. It increases our method coverage of available corpora.

Once the selected NER has returned detected named entities in a text, we only keep the locations. Then, each location is validated by checking their existence in the gazetteer.

4.2 Toponym Resolution

After identifying toponyms in text, we need to associate them with spatial entities. However, toponyms may be linked to different spatial entities *e.g. Paris, France ≠ Paris, Las Vegas*. To select which spatial entity is referred to a toponym in a text, we designed a disambiguation process divided in two parts.

First, we compute a score for each spatial entity candidate for a toponym. Second, we associate the toponym with the spatial entity having the maximum score. However, if the maximum score is not superior to a threshold (fixed to 4 in this use-case), we take the most frequently associated spatial entity for the corresponding toponym *e.g. Paris → Paris, France*. This process is illustrated in Figure 2.

Most Frequently Associated Spatial Entity   If no spatial entity candidate is validated for a toponym, we associate the most frequently used one *e.g. Paris → Paris, France*. In order to do that, we need an "importance" value for each spatial entity. Every spatial entities stored in Geodict are indirectly linked to Wikipedia (using Wikidata). One way of computing popularity of webpage is to compute its page rank (Page et al., 1999). Hence, we decide to assign a page rank (PR) value computed on Wikipedia as proposed in (Thalhammer and Rettinger, 2016) to each spatial entity.

---

[11]http://www.nltk.org/

4.2.1 Score computation

In order to compute the score, we used 4 features associated with each spatial entity in Geodict:

- **P47** This property indicates which entities are adjacent to a corresponding entity. For example, Italy, Spain, U.K., Belgium, Gemany, etc. will be associated with France using P47. However, it does not give adjacency information between two adjacent entities at different (*e.g. country and city*)

- **P131** This property indicates in which administrative territorial entity is included a corresponding spatial entity *e.g. Paris is located in Ile de France.*

- **P706** This property indicates on which terrain feature is included a corresponding spatial entity *e.g. The Statue of Liberty is located on Liberty Island.*

- **Administrative boundaries** Polygon(s) describing administrative boundary(ies) of a spatial entity

For each spatial entity associated with a toponym, we search for existing relationships with the fixed spatial entities[12] in the text. Then each relationship is associated with a weight that denotes its importance. These relationships are using previously mentioned features and their weight are detailed in Table 4.

Relationship	Weight
Adjacency using Boundaries	2
P47 (Share Borders With)	3
Inclusion Score	See Paragraph 4.2.1

Table 4: Impact Weight of Properties on Disambiguations

Each weight is defined from different observations:

- In most cases, spatial relationships based on boundaries polygons are good indicators of the geographical context. However, in particular case, it can also bring confusion. For example, the boundaries between France and Surinam shown in Figure 3.

- As boundaries polygons, the property P47 contains relevant information to the geographical context. However, it contains simpler information (one scale adjacency) but less confusing. Hence, relationships found with P47 are more reliable than boundaries polygons.

- Finally, we considered spatial relationships found using P131 and P706 reliable since they contains precise information on the spatial entities in the spatial hierarchy ($Paris > Ile\ de\ France > France > Europe > Earth$)

Inclusion Score To compute the inclusion score, we compare their inclusion chain made from P131 and P706. An inclusion chain is a list of spatial entities ordered by their inclusion. For example, the inclusion of Coutances and Caen in Figure 4 using P131.

Once inclusion chains using P131 and P706 of the two compared spatial entities are extracted, we compute the size of the intersection between them. For example, the size of the intersection between Caen and Coutances P131 inclusion chains is equal to 2. The inclusion score is defined as the sum of the intersections size of P131 and P706 inclusion chains. However, last spatial entities in inclusion chain are most likely to be equal. Therefore, we are summing the Fibonacci value of each intersection length value. It allows us to lower the impact of low score (resp. increase higher score).

---

[12]Spatial entities which does not share their toponym

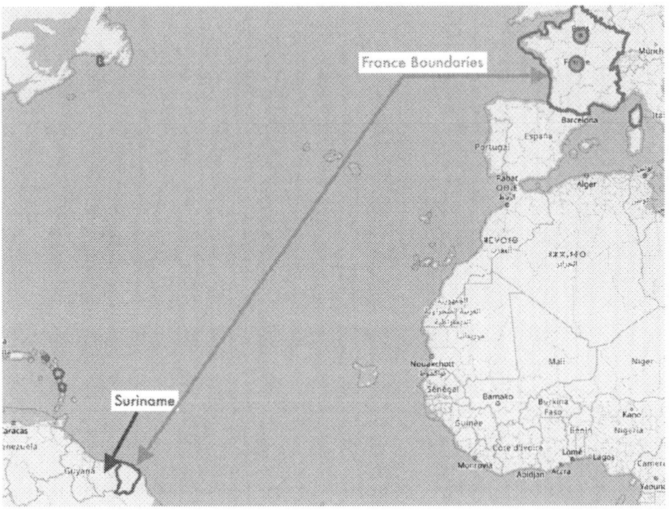

Figure 3: Adjacency Confusion

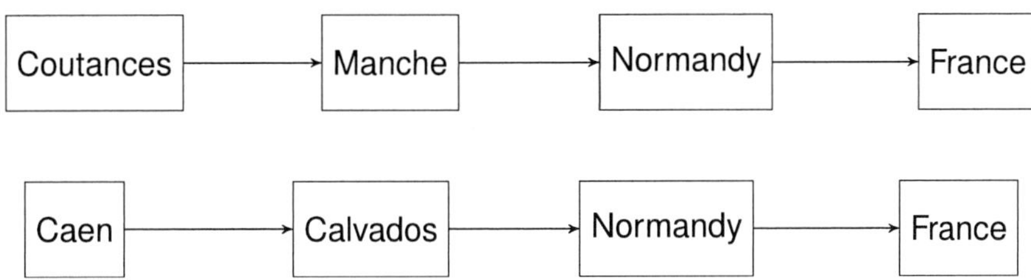

Figure 4: Inclusion chain of Coutances and Caen using P131

Ultimately, we define the inclusion score in Equation 1.

$$inclusion_{score}(se_1, se_2) = fib(|inc(se_1, P_{706}) \cap inc(se_2, P_{706})|) \\ + fib(|inc(se_1, P_{131}) \cap inc(se_2, P_{131})|) \tag{1}$$

with:

- $fib(x)$, Fibonacci value of x

- $inc(se_i, P_y)$, inclusion chain of the spatial entity se_i using the property P_y

4.3 Disambiguation process evaluation

In this paper, we choose to focus on the toponym resolution process. In particular, for each document processed, we run our process on their list of annotated toponyms. Thus, the accuracy measure is the most adapted (Equation 2).

$$Accuracy(TP, SE) = \frac{\sum\limits_{t \in TP, s \in SE} \delta(t, s)}{|TP|} \tag{2}$$

where:

- TP list of toponyms

- SE list of spatial entities associated to each toponym in TP

- $\delta(t, s)$ equal to 1 if the toponym t was correctly associated with s

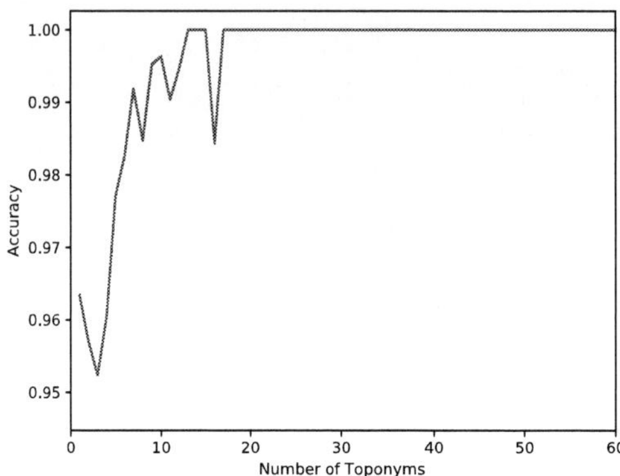

Figure 5: Accuracy evolution over different size of the list of toponyms to disambiguate

In order to evaluate our toponym resolution method, we built a corpus composed of 10000 random documents extracted from Wikipedia.

A Wikipedia article is written using a markup language composed of different tags. Among these tags, anchors allow to link different Wikipedia pages between them. Therefore, if a spatial entity exists in a Wikipedia article, it is referenced using an anchor. However, non-spatial entities can be referenced using these anchors. Thus, we use DBpedia to filter other named entities. In a nutshell, DBpedia is a knowledge base constructed on Wikipedia data including it's URI *e.g.* `http://fr.dbpedia.org/page/Louis_XIV` ⇔ `https://fr.wikipedia.org/wiki/Louis_XIV`. In DBpedia, each entity is associated with a main concept (Location, Person, etc.). Hence, it allows us to filter non spatial entity referenced in anchors for a Wikipedia article.

We obtain good performance with an average accuracy of 95.74% over the 10000 documents. In addition, we highlight our system efficiency over different size of toponym sets to disambiguate, as illustrated in Figure 5.

To strengthen the evaluation, our method could be compared to state-of-the-art methods on recognized corpora such as **TR-CoNLL** introduced in (Leidner, 2007), **LGL** in (Lieberman et al., 2010) or more recently **WarOfTheRebellion** by (DeLozier et al., 2016).

5 Conclusion

In this paper, we propose an integrated gazetteer Geodict that contains basic yet precise geographical information about places names. We conceived it to be multi-purpose by allowing users to customize its creation and link each spatial entity to commonly used datasets. Geodict was used for a geoparsing task and more precisely for toponym resolution. Based on a large corpus, we obtain good results and show the suitability of Geodict.

However, Geodict coverage must be improved by designing new extraction predicates over the different used sources. As for geoparsing, we consider improving our evaluation relevancy by comparing our method to state-of-art methods on referenced corpora.

References

Al-Rfou, R., V. Kulkarni, B. Perozzi, and S. Skiena (2015, April). Polyglot-NER: Massive multilingual named entity recognition. *Proceedings of the 2015 SIAM International Conference on Data Mining, Vancouver, British Columbia, Canada, April 30 - May 2, 2015.*

Anelli, V. W., A. Cal'ı, T. Di Noia, M. Palmonari, and A. Ragone (2016). Exposing open street map in the linked data cloud. In *Trends in Applied Knowledge-Based Systems and Data Science - 29th International Conference on Industrial Engineering and Other Applications of Applied Intelligent Systems, IEA/AIE 2016, Morioka, Japan, August 2-4, 2016, Proceedings*, pp. 344–355.

Barboza, P. (2014, December). *Evaluation of epidemiological intelligence systems applied to the early detection of infectious diseases worldwide.* Theses, Université Pierre et Marie Curie - Paris VI.

Berners-Lee, T., J. Hendler, O. Lassila, et al. (2001). The semantic web. *Scientific american 284*(5), 28–37.

Clough, P., M. Sanderson, and H. Joho (2004). Extraction of semantic annotations from textual web pages. *Deliverable D15 6201.*

DeLozier, G., J. Baldridge, and L. London (2015). Gazetteer-independent toponym resolution using geographic word profiles. In *AAAI*, pp. 2382–2388.

DeLozier, G., B. Wing, J. Baldridge, and S. Nesbit (2016). Creating a novel geolocation corpus from historical texts. *LAW X*, 188.

Finkel, J. R., T. Grenager, and C. Manning (2005). Incorporating non-local information into information extraction systems by gibbs sampling. In *Proceedings of the 43rd annual meeting on association for computational linguistics*, pp. 363–370. Association for Computational Linguistics.

Grossman, D. A. and O. Frieder (2004). *Information Retrieval - Algorithms and Heuristics, Second Edition*, Volume 15 of *The Kluwer International Series on Information Retrieval*. Kluwer.

Hill, L. L. (2000). Core elements of digital gazetteers: placenames, categories, and footprints. In *International Conference on Theory and Practice of Digital Libraries*, pp. 280–290. Springer.

Leidner, J. L. (2007). Toponym resolution in text: annotation, evaluation and applications of spatial grounding. In *ACM SIGIR Forum*, Volume 41, pp. 124–126. ACM.

Li, C. and A. Sun (2014). Fine-grained location extraction from tweets with temporal awareness. In *The 37th International ACM SIGIR Conference on Research and Development in Information Retrieval, SIGIR '14, Gold Coast , QLD, Australia - July 06 - 11, 2014*, pp. 43–52.

Li, H., R. K. Srihari, C. Niu, and W. Li (2003). InfoXtract location normalization. *Proceedings of the HLT-NAACL 2003 workshop on Analysis of geographic references - 1*, 39–44.

Lieberman, M. D., H. Samet, and J. Sankaranarayanan (2010). Geotagging with local lexicons to build indexes for textually-specified spatial data. In *Data Engineering (ICDE), 2010 IEEE 26th International Conference on*, pp. 201–212. IEEE.

Overell, S. and S. Rger (2008). Using cooccurrence models for placename disambiguation. *International Journal of Geographical Information Science 22*(3), 265–287.

Page, L., S. Brin, R. Motwani, and T. Winograd (1999). The pagerank citation ranking: Bringing order to the web. Technical report, Stanford InfoLab.

Rauch, E., M. Bukatin, and K. Baker (2003). A confidence-based framework for disambiguating geographic terms. In *Proceedings of the HLT-NAACL 2003 workshop on Analysis of geographic references-Volume 1*, pp. 50–54. Association for Computational Linguistics.

Stadler, C., J. Lehmann, K. Hffner, and S. Auer (2012). Linkedgeodata: A core for a web of spatial open data. *Semantic Web Journal 3*(4), 333–354.

Thalhammer, A. and A. Rettinger (2016, October). PageRank on Wikipedia: Towards General Importance Scores for Entities. In *The Semantic Web: ESWC 2016 Satellite Events, Heraklion, Crete, Greece, May 29 – June 2, 2016, Revised Selected Papers*, pp. 227–240. Cham: Springer International Publishing.

Vrandečić, D. and M. Krötzsch (2014). Wikidata: a free collaborative knowledgebase. *Communications of the ACM 57*(10), 78–85.

Zenasni, S., E. Kergosien, M. Roche, and M. Teisseire (2016). Extracting new spatial entities and relations from short messages. In *Proceedings of the 8th International Conference on Management of Digital EcoSystems, MEDES 2016, Biarritz, France, November 1-4, 2016*, pp. 189–196.

Fine-grained domain classification of text using TERMIUM Plus

Gabriel Bernier-Colborne, Caroline Barrière, Pierre André Ménard
Centre de recherche informatique de Montréal
g.b.colborne@gmail.com, barrieca@crim.ca, menardpa@crim.ca

Abstract

In this article, we present the use of a term bank for text classification purposes. We developed a supervised text classification approach which takes advantage of the domain-based structure of a term bank, namely TERMIUM Plus, as well as its bilingual content. The goal of the text classification task is to correctly identify the appropriate fine-grained domains of short segments of text in both French and English. We developed a vector space model for this task, which we refer to as the DCVSM (domain classification vector space model). In order to train and evaluate the DCVSM, we generated two new datasets from the open data contained in TERMIUM Plus. Results on these datasets show that the DCVSM compares favourably to five other supervised classification algorithms tested, achieving the highest micro-averaged recall (R@1).

1   Introduction

Text classification is a well-known task in Natural Language Processing, which aims at automatically providing additional document-level metadata (e.g. domain, genre, author). To our knowledge, the curated domain structures found in term banks have never been used to automatically provide metadata describing the fine-grained domains discussed in a given document. This might perhaps be due to the fact that term banks have not been made available as open and free resources until recently, as well as the lack of text data annotated using a term bank's domains as target classes, which is necessary for a supervised classification approach.

Our research was stimulated by the gap mentioned above, and our contribution, highlighted in this paper, is both to provide annotated datasets for fine-grained domain classification of texts, and a classification method that achieves high accuracy. We should say that our first contribution is only possible because of the recent release of the term bank TERMIUM Plus, which contains both the domain structuring information and the short text segments which we use to build our two datasets, one for French and one for English. Our second contribution is a comparison of six different supervised classification algorithms on these datasets, which aims to determine which kind of classifier produces the best results on this task. Among the models we tested, the one which achieves the highest accuracy is a vector space model we developed for this task, which we refer to as the domain classification vector space model (DCVSM).

The datasets are described in Section 2 and the DCVSM is explained in Section 3. The experimental setup and results are presented in Sections 4 and 5. Related work is outlined in Section 6.

2   Datasets generated from Termium

The datasets we created for this research were extracted from TERMIUM Plus®, which we will call simply *Termium* from now on. Termium[1] is a multilingual terminology and linguistic data bank, developed by the Translation Bureau of Canada for over thirty years, but only recently released as open data by the Government of Canada. Since 2014, an open version of Termium Plus is available, with periodic

---

[1] http://open.canada.ca/data/en/dataset/94fc74d6-9b9a-4c2e-9c6c-45a5092453aa

updates. So far, it has not been used much for research on computational linguistics, yet it is a rich resource which can be used for such research in various ways, as we will show.

The latest release of Termium contains data in four languages: English, French, Castilian Spanish, and Portuguese. The datasets presented in this paper were extracted from a 2016 release of Termium, which only included English and French data. The release we used contains about 1.33 million records associated with 2252 domains. An example of a record is shown in Table 1.

	English	**French**
Terms	1. *penalty kick*; 2. *penalty*	1. *coup de pied de réparation*; 2. *coup de pied de pénalité*; 3. *coup de réparation*; 4. *coup de pied de punition*; 5. *tir de réparation*; 6. *tir de punition*; 7. *penalty*; 8. *penalty kick*
Definitions	A kick, unopposed except for the goalkeeper, awarded to sanction a foul committed by a defensive player in his own penalty area.	Coup tiré sans opposition de l'adversaire pour sanctionner une faute commise par un joueur défensif dans sa propre surface de réparation.
Contexts	The referee may award a penalty kick for an infringement of the laws.	Les coups de pied de pénalité et les coups de pied francs sont accordés à l'équipe non fautive à la suite de fautes de [ses] adversaires.
Domains	1. Specialized Vocabulary and Phraseologism of Sports; 2. Soccer (Europe: Football); 3. Rugby	1. Vocabulaire spécialisé et phraséologie des sports; 2. Soccer (Europe : football); 3. Rugby

Table 1: Excerpt from a record in Termium.

To create the datasets used in this research, we first had to process the source files containing the open data of Termium in order to reconstruct its records. The source files are organized by domain, and records belonging to multiple domains are represented by multiple rows, often in different files. Furthermore, the source files do not (currently) indicate which rows belong to the same record (i.e. using some kind of unique record identifier). Therefore, data fusion must be performed to reconstruct the records. The principle used to perform the data fusion is that rows that belong to the same record are identical except for the domain fields. By merging the rows which are identical except for these fields and combining the values found in these fields, we can reconstruct Termium's records. Note that there are exceptions to this rule which produce a small quantity of noise (i.e. mismatches between the records shown in the web version of Termium and the index we created using the source files). Thus the 2 million rows in the source files were aggregated into 1.33 million indexed records, from which we extracted the datasets described below. We have released this data[2] in order to make it easier to reproduce the results reported in this paper, and more generally, to train a classifier using the fine-grained classification of Termium.

As illustrated in Table 1, records in Termium are all linked to at least one domain, and many are linked to 2 domains (31% of records), 3 domains (8%) or more (1%). Records can also contain various kinds of textual supports such as a definition or examples which illustrate the use of a term, known as *contexts*. Termium contains about 170 000 of these contexts in English and 155 000 in French, not counting duplicates. These contexts are meant to illustrate the use of a term, but they sometimes also contain definitional or encyclopedic information about the term. Unlike definitions, which often do not contain the term they define, contexts usually contain an occurrence of one of the synonymous terms on the record, as they are meant to illustrate usage. We created two gold standard datasets by extracting these contexts and their associated domains from Termium, one in English and one in French. We will refer to them as the Termium Context (TC) datasets.

Although the contexts in Termium are supposed to show terms in use, we found out during our experiments that some records contain a context in which none of the record's terms actually occur. Therefore, we defined a procedure to automatically validate each context by checking if it contained at least one of the terms of the record(s) in which it was found. The contexts shown in Table 1 are examples of valid contexts as they contain the terms *penalty kick* and *coup de pied de pénalité*. About 85% of the

---

[2]See https://github.com/crim-ca/LOTKS_2017.

Context	Domain
The use of **Jacobson's organ** is most obvious in snakes. If a strong odour or vibration stimulates a snake, its tongue is flicked in and out rapidly. Each time it is retracted the forked tip touches the opening of **Jacobson's organ** in the roof of the mouth, transmitting any chemical fragments adhering to the tongue.	Reptiles and Amphibians
The rate of speed of a composition or a section thereof, ranging from the slowest to the quickest, as is indicated by **tempo** marks such as largo, adagio, andante, moderato, allegro, presto, prestissimo ...	Musicology
A player is "**onside**" when either of his skates are in physical contact with or on his own side of the line at the instant the puck completely crosses the outer edge of that line regardless of the position of his stick.	Ice Hockey

Table 2: Examples of labeled contexts included in the datasets. Terms in bold are those illustrated by each context.

contexts in each language passed this test.

Some contexts appear on multiple records and are associated with several domains, but most are associated with one or two domains, which are often related by a hierarchical relationship (e.g. *Zoology* and *Reptiles and Amphibians*). We decided to treat the classification task as a single-label classification task, therefore only one domain label was retained for each context. This makes the task more difficult, as only one domain is considered correct when evaluating the predictions of a classifier for a given context, even if that context belongs to multiple, related domains according to Termium. To select a single label for these contexts, we used a frequency-based heuristic which favours less frequent (and perhaps more specific) domains. Subsequently, a minimum class (domain) frequency of 20 was imposed, which removed about 5% of the remaining contexts in each language.

Each instance in the TC datasets comprises a context and a domain label, as shown in Table 2. Statistics on the TC datasets are presented in Table 3. Contexts contain about 40-45 tokens on average, which makes these texts much shorter than those typically used to evaluate text classification, yet longer than a typical query in information retrieval. The number of classes (1376 in English, 1342 in French) is also higher than that of other text classification datasets, such as Reuters-21578[3], which contains 118 classes. Thus, this task can be considered a fine-grained domain classification of short texts.

	English	French
Nb instances	139 327	122 151
Nb classes	1376	1342
Min class freq	20	20
Avg class freq	101.3	91.0
Max class freq	1145	1012
Avg tokens/context	40	45

Table 3: TC Datasets statistics.

3 Domain Classification Vector Space Model

The domain classification vector space model (DCVSM) we developed follows the general principles of vector space models[4]. To predict the domain of a short text, the DCVSM considers the short text as a query and Termium domains as pseudo-documents. The underlying principle is that a Termium domain can be viewed as a document containing all the contexts found in the term bank's records and associated with that domain. The short text can then be classified by computing its similarity to each domain (or pseudo-document). We formally define the DCVSM below as a supervised classifier, and compare it to other classifiers in the following sections.

Let $C = \{c_1, \ldots, c_m\}$ be the set of classes and $F = \{f_1, \ldots, f_n\}$ the set of features. A supervised classifier is trained using a collection X of labelled feature vectors $\langle x, c \rangle$, where $x \in \mathbb{R}^n$ is the feature vector and c is its class. To train the DCVSM, we calculate a matrix W which indicates for each pair

---

[3]See `http://www.daviddlewis.com/resources/testcollections/reuters21578/readme.txt`.

[4]See Manning et al. (2009) for an overview of vector space models, as well as classification algorithms and feature selection techniques used for text classification, including those discussed in this section and most of the classifiers evaluated in Section 5.

(f_i, c_j) the strength of the association between feature f_i and class c_j. In the case of the text classification task addressed in this paper, the features are words and the classes are domains, so each value W_{ij} represents the importance of word f_i in domain c_j. Thus, matrix W is similar to the word-document matrices commonly used for text classification and information retrieval (Salton, 1971), word similarity estimation (Turney and Pantel, 2010), and related tasks. These matrices are typically calculated by counting how many times each word occurs in each document, then weighting these frequencies using a scheme such as tf-idf (Spärck Jones, 1972) or an association measure such as pointwise mutual information (Church and Hanks, 1989).

Matrix W is calculated using the following method. For each pair (f_i, c_j), we sum up the values of feature f_i for each feature vector in the training data that belongs to class c_j, which we will note $T_{f_i c_j}$. This can be formulated as follows: $T_{f_i c_j} = \sum_{\langle x,c \rangle \in X_{c_j}} x_i$. where X_{c_j} is the subset of training instances belonging to class c_j, and x_i is the value of feature f_i in x (e.g. the weighted frequency of a word). This sum is then weighted to estimate the association between the feature and the class: $W_{ij} = \psi(T_{f_i c_j})$, where ψ is some weighting function. The resulting value W_{ij} is the weight of feature f_i for class c_j.

Each column vector $W_{.j}$ represents the feature weights of the classifier for class c_j. A new feature vector x is classified by calculating the dot product of x and the feature weights of each class, and selecting the class which maximises this function. In other words, $W_{.j}$ represents a pseudo-document corresponding to domain c_j, and contexts are classified by finding the most similar pseudo-document. Formally, the probability of a class c_j is defined as follows: $\Pr(c_j|x) \propto \sum_{i=1}^{n} x_i W_{ij}$.

The DCVSM assumes that the contribution of each feature to the likelihood of a class is independent of the other features. Many other classifiers make this assumption, including the multinomial Naive Bayes classifier which is often used for text classification. Furthermore, like Naive Bayes, the DCVSM is fast, scalable, and simple to train, as training only involves calculating matrix W on the training data. Naive Bayes is one of the five classifiers to which we compare the DCVSM in the following experiment.

4   Text classification experiment

Using the TC datasets (in English and French) described in Section 2, we evaluated the DCVSM as well as five other supervised classification algorithms that have been used for text classification. Each short text (instance) from a TC dataset was converted into a bag of words after applying basic preprocessing (tokenization, lemmatization, case-folding, and removal of stop words and punctuation)[5]. Thus, each instance is represented by a feature vector where each value is the frequency of a specific word. The set of features contains every word that occurs at least twice in the training data. Word frequencies were optionally weighted using tf-idf, with idf being defined as follows for a given word w: $\mathrm{idf}(w) = \log\left(\frac{|D|}{|D_w|} + 1\right)$, where D is the set of contexts used for training, $|D|$ is its size, and D_w is the subset of training contexts that contain w.

The five other supervised classification algorithms we tested are: multinomial Naive Bayes (NB), Rocchio classification (RC), softmax regression (SR), k-nearest neighbours (k-NN) and a multi-layer perceptron (MLP).

As noted above, multinomial Naive Bayes is commonly used for text classification. Rocchio classification (Rocchio, 1971), like Naive Bayes, is a linear classification algorithm. The DCVSM is similar to Rocchio classification, which involves computing centroids by averaging all the feature vectors belonging to each class, and classifying new instances by assigning them to the class of the nearest centroid. The DCVSM is different in that the feature vectors belonging to each class are summed rather than being averaged, and then weighted.

Softmax regression (or multinomial logistic regression) is also a linear classification algorithm. The softmax classifier was trained using stochastic gradient descent, with a penalty on the L2 norm of the feature weights for regularisation.

---

[5]Stanford's CoreNLP library (Manning et al., 2014) was used for tokenization. TreeTagger (Schmid, 1994) and TT4J (`https://reckart.github.io/tt4j/tokenizer.html`) were used for lemmatization.

The k-NN algorithm and the MLP are non-linear classifiers. k-NN classifies a given instance based on the classes of the k most similar instances in the training data. The MLP is also known as a fully connected artificial neural network. A description of artificial neural networks and the backpropagation algorithm used to train them can be found in Rumelhart et al. (1986), and Bengio (2012) provides a practical guide to training and tuning neural networks. We tested MLPs containing 1 or 2 hidden layers of exponential linear units (Clevert et al., 2015). The MLP was trained using the Adam algorithm (Kingma and Ba, 2014) and regularised using dropout and a max-norm constraint on the incoming weights of all units (Srivastava et al., 2014).

Each TC dataset was split into 3 subsets of equal size (about 46K instances in English and 41K in French) for training, validation, and testing. A grid search was used to tune the hyperparameters of each classifier on the validation set (except Naive Bayes, which has no hyperparameters). Then the best configuration of each classifier was evaluated on the held-out test set. Each classifier was tuned and tested twice, once using raw word frequencies as input, and once using tf-idf weighted frequencies. The impact of this weighting will be assessed in the next section.

For the DCVSM, the only hyperparameter is the weighting scheme ψ used to compute the feature weights. We tested nine different weighting schemes including tf-idf[6] and the simple association measures defined in Evert (2007, ch. 4). These association measures compare the observed frequency of (word, context) pairs to their expected frequency in order to measure the strength of their association. We calculate this expectation using the following equation:

$$\mathbb{E}[T_{f_i c_j}] = \frac{\sum_{j'=1}^{m} T_{f_i c_{j'}} \sum_{i'=1}^{n} T_{f_{i'} c_j}}{\sum_{i'=1}^{n} \sum_{j'=1}^{m} T_{f_{i'} c_{j'}}}$$

where $T_{f_i c_j}$, as defined earlier (see Section 3), is the sum, for each feature vector in the training data belonging to class c_j, of the value of feature f_i. We set all of the association measures to 0 if $T_{f_i c_j} <= \mathbb{E}[T_{f_i c_j}]$. We optionally apply a log or square root transformation to the output of all the weighting schemes, following Lapesa et al. (2014).

For Rocchio classification, we tuned the measure used to estimate the distance between a feature vector and the class centroids (euclidean distance or cosine). For k-NN, we tuned the number of neighbours (k) and the distance-based weighting of neighbours. For the softmax classifier, we tuned the learning rate and the L2 penalty coefficient. As for the MLP, we tuned the number of hidden layers (1 or 2), the number of units in each, the learning rate, the number of training iterations (epochs), the dropout probability and the max-norm constraint.

5   Results

Table 4 shows the accuracy achieved by each classifier on the test sets in English and French. Accuracy is measured using two different evaluation measures, namely micro-averaged recall at rank 1 (R@1) and recall at rank 5 (R@5). R@1 is simply the percentage of correctly classified instances. This is the measure that was used to tune the models on the validation set. It only considers the top prediction of a classifier for a given test case, whereas R@5 considers the top five predictions. In other words, R@5 is the percentage of test cases for which the correct class is among the five most likely classes according to the classifier.

The results indicate that the DCVSM achieves a higher R@1 than the five other classifiers tested, and the second-highest R@5, just behind the MLP. The DCVSM does not fit the training data as well as other classifiers, yet it achieves the highest R@1 on the held-out data used for testing. The MLP can easily fit the training data perfectly (as can k-NN), which the DCVSM cannot. Regularisation techniques (dropout, max-norm constraint, early stopping) were used to avoid overfitting the training data using the MLP, yet no configuration we tested scored better on the validation data (in terms of R@1) than

---

[6]Not to be confused with the tf-idf weighting that is optionally applied to the input feature vectors. Here, tf-idf is applied to the feature weight vectors of each class (as the weighting scheme ψ), rather than the feature vectors of each instance in the dataset.

	R@1		R@5	
	EN	**FR**	**EN**	**FR**
k-NN	0.104	0.080	0.107	0.085
NB	0.224	0.218	0.442	0.430
SR	0.245	0.241	0.494	0.476
RC	0.253	0.253	0.504	0.498
MLP	0.264	0.260	**0.530**	**0.521**
DCVSM	**0.283**	**0.277**	0.529	0.512

Table 4: Micro-averaged R@1 and R@5 on the test sets in English and French.

	Δ R@1		Δ R@5	
	EN	**FR**	**EN**	**FR**
k-NN	-0.016	+0.005	-0.016	+0.005
NB	+0.051	+0.072	+0.085	+0.140
SR	+0.016	+0.020	+0.034	+0.042
RC	+0.066	+0.108	+0.122	+0.198
MLP	-0.005	-0.002	-0.006	-0.005
DCVSM	-0.008	-0.002	-0.007	-0.001

Table 5: Impact of weighting the feature values using tf-idf.

the DCVSM. It remains possible that higher accuracy could be achieved using an MLP by testing other regularisation or optimisation techniques. It is also possible that the DCVSM could produce even higher accuracy if we tested other weighting schemes.

The scores shown in Table 4 represent the best of two scores for each classifier, using either raw word frequencies or tf-idf weighted frequencies as input. Table 5 shows the impact of using tf-idf to weight the word frequencies on the accuracy achieved by each classifier on the test sets. These results show that the DCVSM performs slightly better when feature values are raw word frequencies, as does the MLP. Other classifiers perform much worse when the input is not weighted using tf-idf, especially the Naive Bayes and Rocchio classifiers.

To gain insight on both the datasets and the DCVSM, we inspected the classes on which the DCVSM achieved the lowest and highest recall. The classes for which recall was highest on the test set in English are shown in Table 6, along with the top features for each of these classes, most of which do seem like good predictors for these classes.

Class	R@1	Top features
Solid Fuel Heating	1.000	stoker, grate, chain-grate, stokers, traveling-grate, underfeed, pulverize, pulverizer, direct-fired, coal, ...
Opening and Closing Devices (Packaging)	0.900	press-on, closure, dauber, innerseal, cap, foil, applicator, ct, heat-sealed, hermetic, ...
Hats and Millinery	0.900	hat, brim, bicorne, chinstrap, milliner, tricorne, courtier, gentleman, cock, napoleon, ...
Tunnels Overpasses and Bridges	0.880	bridge, span, anchorage, abutment, pontoon, girder, cantilever, pier, 700-m, bridges, ...
Electoral Systems and Political Parties	0.875	election, ballot, electoral, elector, voting, polling, vote, voter, candidate, officer, ...
Deep Foundations	0.867	pile, caisson, pier, hammer, excavation, fuel-injection, morris, concrete, piling, pinning, ...
Yoga and Pilates	0.864	yoga, chakra, bandha, muladhara, pranayama, vinyasa, pose, bhedana, chakras, meditation, ...

Table 6: High-recall classes and their top features.

As for the low-recall classes, inspecting the top features did not provide any clues as to why recall was lower on these classes. However, observing the top prediction for these classes suggests that class frequency and domain granularity are important factors. This is illustrated in Table 7, which shows a few low-recall classes, along with the most frequently predicted class for each of these classes. These pairs of classes show that some distinctions between domains are quite fine-grained. Furthermore, looking at their respective frequencies (shown in brackets) suggests a tendency to predict higher-frequency classes for these low-recall classes.

Predicted class	Correct class
Radio Transmission and Reception [54]	Radio Interference [10]
Criminology [61]	Criminal Psychology [14]
Advertising [46]	Advertising Techniques [31]
Human Behaviour [55]	Animal Behaviour [48]
Artificial Intelligence [383]	Philosophy (General) [21]

Table 7: Low-recall classes (right) and the classes with which they are most often confused (left). The frequency of each class is shown in brackets. This is their frequency in the training set (in English).

An analysis of class-wise recall with respect to class frequency confirmed that recall is systematically lower on low-frequency classes. If we compare the classifiers using macro-averaged (rather than micro-averaged) R@1, i.e. the average R@1 per class across all classes, we obtain the results shown in Table 8. The DCVSM performs better in this respect than every other algorithm except Rocchio classification. It is important to remember that the models were tuned by optimizing micro-averaged R@1, and that optimizing macro-averaged R@1 would produce different results.

Classifier	EN	FR
k-NN	0.082	0.063
NB	0.129	0.127
SR	0.163	0.157
RC	**0.235**	**0.232**
MLP	0.191	0.187
DCVSM	0.230	0.224

Table 8: Macro-averaged R@1.

6   Related Work

We have outlined similarities between the DCVSM presented in this paper and other classification algorithms in section 3. It is worth noting that the DCVSM is related to methods such as explicit semantic analysis or ESA (Gabrilovich and Markovitch, 2007). In ESA, texts are represented in a high-dimensional space of explicit concepts or categories, based on associations between words and these categories. These associations are calculated on some knowledge base, typically Wikipedia, using tf-idf. The main difference between this and the DCVSM presented in this paper is that ESA computes feature weights (i.e. word-category associations) using category-labeled Wikipedia articles as training data.

Mohammad and Hirst (2006) compute associations between words and categories for disambiguation purposes, which are similar to the word-domain associations discussed in this paper. Mohammad and Hirst (2006) calculate these associations using unlabelled text and a thesaurus, whereas we use labeled text, which renders the bootstrapping procedure they propose unnecessary, as the relevant domains of each text are known.

Also worth mentioning is the text classification algorithm introduced by Navigli et al. (2011), which exploits the structure of WordNet (Fellbaum, 1998) and is used to identify the domain of a document. This is evaluated on a (single label) dataset of domain-labelled Wikipedia articles. For reference, they obtain a micro-averaged R@1 of 0.670, which is more than twice as high as the maximum obtained on the task tackled in this paper. However, the articles in their dataset are much longer than the contexts in Termium, the number of domains (29) is smaller by two orders of magnitude, and the prior probabilities of the domains are uniform. The fine-grained nature of the domain classification presented in this paper makes the task more difficult, as does the short length of the texts.

7   Concluding remarks and future work

In this paper, we showed that the fine-grained domain information found in a term bank could be used as a text classification system. We presented domain-labeled datasets generated from the usage contexts found in Termium. We then compared six supervised text classification algorithms on these datasets, including a vector space model we developed for this task, the DCVSM. Results showed that the DCVSM performed well, achieving the highest micro-averaged recall (R@1) and the second-highest macro-averaged recall.

Future work will focus on applications of the DCVSM and the TC datasets. In particular, we wish to go back to the work described in Barrière et al. (2016) and further evaluate the DCVSM on a disambiguation task. The fact that the DCVSM can identify the domain of a short text with relatively high accuracy, as shown in this paper, can be useful in itself, but this information can also be used to disambiguate the words or terms that appear in the text. Domain-driven disambiguation methods first identify the relevant domains of the context in which an ambiguous term (or word) occurs, then use this domain information to identify the sense conveyed by that term in that context. Some methods based on domain identification have been used for word sense disambiguation in Magnini et al. (2001); Gliozzo et al. (2005); Navigli et al. (2011). In our own previous work (Barrière et al., 2016), we performed domain-driven term sense disambiguation, but the disambiguation algorithm exploited a different text classifier. In future work, we plan on measuring the impact of using the higher-accuracy text classifier presented here within our term disambiguation algorithm.

In a more general perspective, we could investigate how representing texts using the fine-grained domain classification of Termium would impact performance on other tasks. Classifying a text using this classification produces a score for each domain, indicating the likelihood that the text is related to that domain. This list of scores can be considered a representation of the text in a high-dimensional space of domains. Representing texts in this domain space could be useful for other classification or clustering purposes, with different applications in mind. We hope our research will help promote the use of terminological resources for such diverse NLP applications. With this in mind, we have made the datasets we developed available to the research community.

Acknowledgments

This research was carried out as part of the PACTE project (Ménard and Barrière, 2017), and was supported by CANARIE and the *ministère de l'Éconnomie, de la Science et de l'Innovation* (MESI) of the Government of Québec.

References

Barrière, C., P. A. Ménard, and D. Azoulay (2016). Contextual term equivalent search using domain-driven disambiguation. In *Proceedings of the 5th International Workshop on Computational Terminology (CompuTerm 2016)*, pp. 21–29.

Bengio, Y. (2012). Practical recommendations for gradient-based training of deep architectures. *CoRR abs/1206.5533*.

Church, K. W. and P. Hanks (1989). Word association norms, mutual information, and lexicography. In *Proceedings of the 27th Annual Meeting of the Association for Computational Linguistics*, pp. 76–83.

Clevert, D., T. Unterthiner, and S. Hochreiter (2015). Fast and accurate deep network learning by exponential linear units (elus). *CoRR abs/1511.07289*.

Evert, S. (2007). Corpora and collocations (extended manuscript). In A. Lüdeling and M. Kytö (Eds.), *Corpus Linguistics. An International Handbook*, Volume 2. Berlin/New York: Walter de Gruyter.

Fellbaum, C. (1998). *WordNet: An Electronic Lexical Database*. Bradford Books.

Gabrilovich, E. and S. Markovitch (2007). Computing semantic relatedness using Wikipedia-based explicit semantic analysis. In *Proceedings of the 20th International Joint Conference on Artificial Intelligence (IJCAI)*, pp. 1606–1611.

Gliozzo, A., C. Giuliano, and C. Strapparava (2005). Domain kernels for word sense disambiguation. In *Proceedings of the 43rd Annual Meeting of the Association for Computational Linguistics (ACL)*, pp. 403–410. ACL.

Kingma, D. P. and J. Ba (2014). Adam: A method for stochastic optimization. *CoRR abs/1412.6980.*

Lapesa, G., S. Evert, and S. Schulte im Walde (2014). Contrasting syntagmatic and paradigmatic relations: Insights from distributional semantic models. In *Proceedings of the Third Joint Conference on Lexical and Computational Semantics (*SEM 2014)*, pp. 160–170. ACL/DCU.

Magnini, B., C. Strapparava, G. Pezzulo, and A. Gliozzo (2001). Using domain information for word sense disambiguation. In *Proceedings of the Second International Workshop on Evaluating Word Sense Disambiguation Systems*, pp. 111–114. ACL.

Manning, C. D., P. Raghavan, and H. Schütze (2009). *Introduction to Information Retrieval (online edition)*. Cambridge University Press.

Manning, C. D., M. Surdeanu, J. Bauer, J. Finkel, S. J. Bethard, and D. McClosky (2014). The Stanford CoreNLP natural language processing toolkit. In *Proceedings of the 52nd Annual Meeting of the Association for Computational Linguistics (ACL): System Demonstrations*, pp. 55–60.

Mohammad, S. and G. Hirst (2006). Determining word sense dominance using a thesaurus. In *Proceedings of the Eleventh Conference of the European Chapter of the Association for Computational Linguistics (EACL)*, pp. 121–128. ACL.

Ménard, P. A. and C. Barrière (2017). PACTE: A collaborative platform for textual annotation. In *13th Joint ISO-ACL Workshop on Interoperable Semantic Annotation (ISA-13)*.

Navigli, R., S. Faralli, A. Soroa, O. de Lacalle, and E. Agirre (2011). Two birds with one stone: learning semantic models for text categorization and word sense disambiguation. In *Proceedings of the 20th ACM International Conference on Information and Knowledge Management*, pp. 2317–2320. ACM.

Rocchio, J. J. (1971). Relevance feedback in information retrieval. See Salton (1971).

Rumelhart, D. E., G. E. Hinton, and R. J. Williams (1986). Learning representations by back-propagating errors. *Nature 323*, 533–536.

Salton, G. (Ed.) (1971). *The SMART Retrieval System – Experiments in Automatic Document Processing*. Prentice Hall.

Schmid, H. (1994). Probabilistic part-of-speech tagging using decision trees. In *Proceedings of the International Conference on New Methods in Language Processing*.

Spärck Jones, K. (1972). A statistical interpretation of term specificity and its application in retrieval. *Journal of documentation 28*(1), 11–21.

Srivastava, N., G. E. Hinton, A. Krizhevsky, I. Sutskever, and R. Salakhutdinov (2014). Dropout: a simple way to prevent neural networks from overfitting. *Journal of Machine Learning Research 15*(1), 1929–1958.

Turney, P. D. and P. Pantel (2010). From frequency to meaning: Vector space models of semantics. *Journal of Artificial Intelligence Research 37*(1), 141–188.

TBX in ODD: Schema-agnostic specification and documentation for TermBase eXchange

Stefan Pernes
INRIA
stefan.pernes@inria.fr

Laurent Romary
INRIA
laurent.romary@inria.fr

Kara Warburton
Termologic
kara@termologic.com

Abstract

TermBase eXchange (TBX), the ISO standard for the representation and interchange of terminological data, is currently undergoing revision and will for the first time formalize overarching structural constraints regarding the definition and validation of dialects and XML styles. The paper describes the design of an ODD architecture, which allows for a complete specification of present-day TBX.

1 Introduction

TermBase eXchange (TBX), the ISO standard for the representation and interchange of terminological data, is currently undergoing revision and will for the first time formalize overarching structural constraints regarding the definition and validation of dialects and XML styles. To match these requirements, the ODD specification language provides advanced subset selection and constraint specification capabilities covering both structure and content of text encoding formalisms. Following the literate programming methodology, it furthermore allows the definition of integrated resources, which contain formal specifications alongside their prose descriptions and usage examples. This paper first describes the meta-model behind TBX as well as current challenges in the context of its revision. From this follows a description of applicable ODD mechanisms and the design of an ODD architecture, which allows for a complete specification of present-day TBX.

2 Terminological Markup Framework and TermBase eXchange

Terminology standards have witnessed a long evolution since 1987 when a first pre-SGML format for storage and interchange via magnetic tapes was devised. Published in 2003 as ISO 16642 (2003), the Terminological Markup Framework (TMF) marks a pivotal point in the succession of terminology standards as it constitutes a meta structure for terminology encoding which also provides the foundation for the more recent TBX format. TMF *specifies a framework designed to provide guidance on the basic principles for representing data recorded in terminological data collections* (ibid.). Its aims can be described as twofold (Romary 2001, 2f): (1) as a meta-model for terminological data representation it facilitates the description and comparison of existing interchange formats, and (2) it provides a mechanism for the flexible definition of interchange formats while safeguarding interoperability between them. The specification of such a meta-model thus eases the integration of different terminological databases with each other as well as with other lexical resources. In principle, TMF allows one to describe a potentially infinite set of Terminological Markup Languages (TML). Formally, this flexibility is achieved by describing the various components of terminological databases as either part of the structural skeleton or as data categories. This leads to the four elementary notions of TMF (ibid., 3f):

1. The meta-model: A structural skeleton for terminological entries following a concept-oriented, or onomasiological, view.

2. Information units taken from a Data Category Repository (DCR) as described in ISO 12620 (1999) (a new version is about to be published).

3. Methods and representations: The actual implementation of a TML, combining the structural skeleton with the chosen data categories. This also comprises the mappings between data categories and the vocabularies used to express them (e.g. as an XML element or a database field).

4. A generic mapping tool: A methodology that maps any given TML onto the meta-model. The notion of a generic mapping tool can be replaced by the ODD architecture as proposed in this paper.

As a consequence of these elementary notions, the interoperability between two TMLs is reduced to a comparison of their respective use of data categories.

TermBase eXchange (TBX) as defined by ISO 30042 (2008) is precisely an instantiation of the described meta-model alongside a specific selection of data categories. It is a reference implementation of TMF, taking the form of XML (thus its official specification is implemented as XML DTD, RelaxNG, and W3C schemas) and constituting what is nowadays called TBX-Default, or the master TBX dialect. It is *designed to support various types of processes involving terminological data, including analysis, descriptive representation, dissemination, and interchange (exchange), in various computer environments* (ibid.). TBX is currently undergoing extensive review as ISO CD30042 (2017): It establishes provisions for the specification of official TBX dialects, such as their minimum requirements in terms of structure and data categories. Furthermore, it is targeting increased interoperability by merging the content models of two alternative term information group elements, *tig* and *ntig*, into one *termSec* element. See Figure 1 for a short sample TBX entry (in accordance with the current Community Draft version). Additionally, two markup styles, data categories as tags (DCT) and data categories as attribute values (DCA), are defined. Apart from the need for a modular framework for dialect specification, a consequence of this development is that the specification of TBX itself will profit from tighter control over data categories, their identifiers and values, as well as data type information for these values. As has also been noted in the context of data exchange with Linked Open Data description formalisms such as RDF and OWL, the current specification of TBX does not provide data type description mechanisms in the classical sense, focussing mostly on string values based on W3C XML primitives (cf. Reineke 2014, 7). Thus, the strengths of an ODD architecture as proposed herein are a modular mechanism for the description of TBX dialects and an increased control over data types.

3 The Text Encoding Initiative and *One Document Does it all*

The Text Encoding Initiative (TEI) maintains a set of guidelines which have become a de facto standard in the encoding of literary, historical, and linguistics research data. Being established in 1987, the TEI guidelines predate and inform a number of modern web and encoding standards. They comprise close to 500 elements which are organised in functional-thematic modules, classes of shared attributes, and macros for common content models. The broadness and complexity of the TEI is paired with its own specification language that allows for a modular definition of project-specific customizations. One Document Does it all (ODD) is a generic specification language, establishing a separation between the specification of TEI encoding models and current schema languages, be it a XML DTD, a RelaxNG schema, or a W3C schema. Thus, TEI encoding models are essentially agnostic about the choice of a representation language and could also map to formalisms other than XML (Burnard 2013, 13). Furthermore, ODD follows the literate programming paradigm and constitutes a single resource containing formal declarations alongside descriptive prose and examples of usage (Burnard and Rahtz 2004, 3). Figure 2 schematically displays the different aspects of processing ODD files.

```xml
 1  <conceptEntry id="c45">
 2      <transacGrp>
 3          <transactionType>origination</transactionType>
 4          <responsibility target="pe324as3-9615-4d41-a9c8-30c36bffe0e6">Tommy</responsibility>
 5      </transacGrp>
 6      <subjectField>General</subjectField>
 7      <xGraphic target="Black_Dwarf.jpg">Black_Dwarf.jpg</xGraphic>
 8      <note>G-Source: http://www.dorlingkindersley-uk.co.uk/static/clipart/uk/dk/sci_space/image_sci_space013.jpg</note>
 9      <langSec xml:lang="en">
10          <transacGrp>
11              <transactionType>origination</transactionType>
12              <responsibility target="pe324as3-9615-4d41-a9c8-30c36bffe0e6">Tommy</responsibility>
13          </transacGrp>
14          <descripGrp>
15              <definition>A degenerate star that has cooled until it is no longer visible.</definition>
16              <source>Oxford2007</source>
17          </descripGrp>
18          <termSec>
19              <term>black dwarf</term>
20              <partOfSpeech>noun</partOfSpeech>
21              <descripGrp>
22                  <context>Banprupt though it is, a white swarf still has a high surface temperature when it is first formed; up to 100,000
23                      radiate. Gradually it fades, and must end up as a cold, dead black dwarf; but at the moment no white dwarf with a surf
24                      found, and it may be that the universe is not yet old enough for any black dwarfs to have been formed.</context>
25                  <source>Moore2003, 173</source>
26              </descripGrp>
27          </termSec>
28      </langSec>
29      <langSec xml:lang="es"> [25 lines]
55  </conceptEntry>
```

Figure 1: Example TBX entry in DCT style

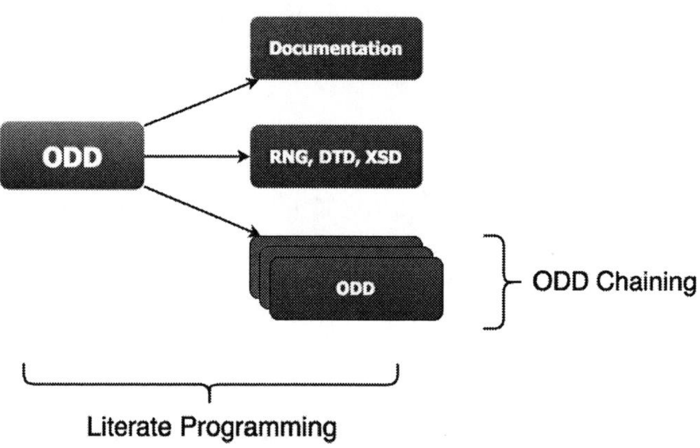

Figure 2: ODD processing and chaining

certainty	count	duration.iso	duration.w3c	enumerated
interval	language	name	namespace	namespaceOrName
nullOrName	numeric	outputMeasurement	pattern	percentage
point	pointer	prefix	probability	probCert
replacement	sex	temporal.iso	temporal.w3c	text
truthValue	unboundedInt	version	versionNumber	word
xmlName	xpath	xTruthValue		

Figure 3: TEI datatypes

Formal declarations in ODD concern foremost the key components of the TEI abstract model: elements, attributes, modules, classes, and macros. The last three components serve to reduce the overall systems complexity and allow a coarse-grained selection of characteristics for a TEI customization. Another major simplification stems from a conscious effort to provide uniform levels of description and hence processing allowing components to be added, changed, replaced, or deleted within a given context and at any point in a schema declaration (Burnard and Rahtz 2004, 8). Modifications of this kind can be chained together (ODD chaining), thus making it easy to supplement a broadly specified TEI customization with fine-grained, context-specific modifications. The context specificity of such declarations also allows for a tighter constraint on possible attribute values by means of data typing (Burnard 2013, 10): The vast majority of attribute values are defined by reference to a data type macro as defined within the ODD system, which are in turn mapped to a W3C Schema data type or to an expression in RELAX NG syntax, thus allowing the ODD system to overlay additional semantics onto such bare data types (see Figure 3, TEI datatypes). Additionally, a further layer of constraint specification can be added using ISO Schematron, making it possible to implement many of the informally expressed rules for good practice, which are typically found in the prose of encoding guidelines.

4   Description of the *TBX in ODD* architecture

Prior work has already established an ODD architecture for the ISO 30042 (2008) *Basic* dialect (Romary 2014). Furthermore, the TBX specification published in 2008 was actually written in ODD by the core editorial team of the time[1]. This approach – a major diversion from conventional ISO authoring practices – was undertaken as case study for the use of ODD to author ISO standards that contain a mixture of prose, machine-readable specifications and sample code, and that require schemas as derivative products. Major changes introduced by the current revision of TBX are a modular framework for the specification of dialects and the implementation of markup styles (DCA vs. DCT). Both requirements can be met via module selection in ODD. A prerequisite for this ODD chaining mechanism is a master ODD file, containing specifications for all core structure elements and permissible data categories (it is equivalent to TBX-Default, the so-called master TBX dialect). Specifying a new TBX dialect in ODD is achieved by selecting modules and classes, or parts thereof, and selecting data categories from the ISO Data Category Repository, which may also extend on the TBX default set of data categories. Using the ODD framework, this dialect can afterwards be transformed into any of the supported schema languages for document validation – which also serve as the official specification of TBX and its dialects. The same approach applies for the validation of one or the other data category style. For example, in order to generate a schema for validating files using only DCA style, one would define a subset of the master ODD that excludes the module *TBXDCT* and vice versa.

A preliminary overview of the module and class organization is shown in Figure 4. File header elements, core structure, and elements specific to the two markup styles are grouped into modules, while

---

[1] Arle Lommel, Alan Melby, and Kara Warburton

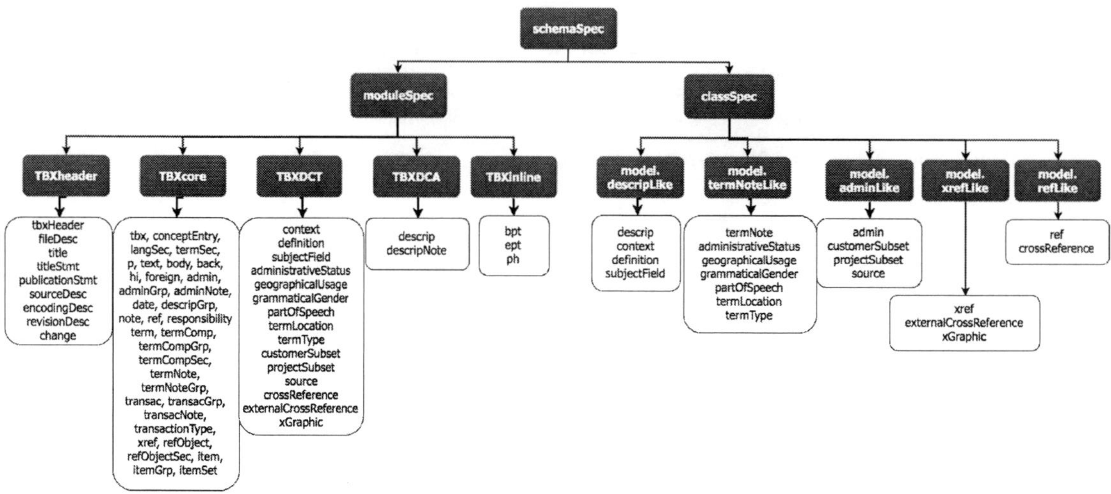

Figure 4: TBX module and class organization in ODD

elements with similar content models are grouped into classes. The interlocking nature of the organization hints at the powerful subset selection mechanism. As the revision of TBX is still ongoing, some data category and constraint specifications are yet to be implemented.

5 Conclusion

In this paper we have described the specification of TermBase eXchange (TBX), which is currently undergoing revision as ISO CD30042 (2017), using the ODD specification language. The requirements for this upcoming version of TBX include a system for the derivation of dialects, which need to be verifiably compliant to the core structure and, in the best case, can be defined in a user-friendly, modular fashion. The ODD language provides such a framework and follows a literate programming approach where documentation, usage examples, and formal specifications all reside in one document. Additionally, it is a sustainable approach that does not depend on any specific schema language and is in principle able to map to the data modelling ecosystem of the day – an advantage given the long-term perspective of terminology encoding standards.

References

Burnard, L. (2013). Resolving the Durand Conundrum. *Journal of the Text Encoding Initiative 6.* `http://jtei.revues.org/842`.

Burnard, L. and S. Rahtz (2004). RelaxNG with son of ODD. *Extreme Markup Languages.* `http://www.tei-c.org/cms/Talks/extreme2004/paper.html`.

ISO 12620 (1999). Terminology and other language and content resources – Specification of data categories and management of a Data Category Registry for language resources. Standard, International Organization for Standardization, Geneva, Switzerland.

ISO 16642 (2003). Computer applications in terminology – Terminological markup framework. Standard, International Organization for Standardization, Geneva, Switzerland.

ISO 30042 (2008). Systems to manage terminology, knowledge and content – TermBase eXchange (TBX). Standard, International Organization for Standardization, Geneva, Switzerland.

ISO CD30042 (2017). Systems to manage terminology, knowledge and content – TermBase eXchange (TBX). Standard, International Organization for Standardization, Geneva, Switzerland.

Reineke, D. (2014). TBX between termbases and ontologies. *Proceedings of the 11th International Conference on Terminology and Knowledge Engineering, TKE 2014.* `http://hal.archives-ouvertes.fr/hal-01005838`.

Romary, L. (2001). An abstract model for the representation of multilingual terminological data: TMF – Terminological Markup Framework. *Proceedings of the 5th TermNet Symposium, TAMA 2001.* `http://hal.inria.fr/inria-00100405`.

Romary, L. (2014). TBX goes TEI – Implementing a TBX basic extension for the Text Encoding Initiative guidelines. *Proceedings of the 11th International Conference on Terminology and Knowledge Engineering, TKE 2014.* `hal-00950862v2`.

Enrichment of French Biomedical Ontologies with UMLS Concepts and Semantic Types for Biomedical Named Entity Recognition Though Ontological Semantic Annotation.

Andon Tchechmedjiev

Université de Montpellier, LIRMM

andon.tchechmedjiev@lirmm.fr

Clément Jonquet

Université de Monpellier, LIRMM

Center for Biomedical Informatics Research,

Stanford University

jonquet@lirmm.fr

September 6, 2017

Abstract

Medical terminologies and ontologies are a crucial resource for semantic annotation of biomedical text. In French, there are considerably less resources and tools to use them than in English. Some terminologies from the Unified Medical Language System have been translated but often the identifiers used in the UMLS Metathesaurus, that make its huge integrated value, have been lost during the process. In this work, we present our method and results in enriching seven French versions of UMLS sources with UMLS Concept Unique Identifiers and Semantic Types based on information extracted from class labels, multilingual translation mappings and codes. We then measure the impact of the enrichment through the application of the SIFR Annotator, a service to identify ontology concepts in free text deployed within the SIFR BioPortal, a repository for French biomedical ontologies and terminologies. We use the Quaero Corpus to evaluate.

1   Introduction

As of early 2017, the Linked Open Data cloud diagram[1] became largely dominated by life-sciences and more specifically, by biomedical ontologies and terminologies hosted on the BioPortal repository developed by the US National Center for Biomedical Ontology (Noy et al., 2009). The NCBO BioPortal, is a reference ontology repository for the biomedical domain that provides open and accessible ontology indexing, browsing, search recommendation and semantic annotation. NCBO BioPortal includes, as of Summer 2017, more than 580 language resources, but only few are not in English, e.g., five in French and one in Spanish (Jonquet et al., 2015). Furthermore, the UMLS (Unified Medical Language System) Metathesaurus (Bodenreider, 2004), even if it covers 21 languages, 75.1% of its terms are in English and only 1.82% of its terms are in French (Bollegala et al., 2015).

Our work is part of the SIFR project (Semantic Indexing of French Biomedical Data Resources - http://www.lirmm.fr/sifr) in which we are interested in exploiting ontologies in construction of services like indexing, mining, and information retrieval for French biomedical resources. In this project, we develop a semantic indexing workflow (called the French/SIFR Annotator) based on ontologies similar to that existing for English resources [16], but focused on the French resources. The present study concerns 7 French terminologies hosted on the SIFR BioPortal (http://BioPortal.lirmm.fr) (a local instance of

---

BioPortal dedicated to French) that we wished to formally enrich with UMLS concepts and semantic type identifiers.

To improve the SIFR Annotator workflow and enable the use of UMLS identifiers, we present our method and results in enriching seven French medical terminologies with UMLS Concept Unique Identifiers (CUIs) and Semantic Type identifiers (TUIs). The English version of the seven processed terminologies are included within the UMLS Metathesaurus, but the original concept and type identifiers have not been ported to their French version, when translated. This was a big limitation for users interested in manipulating the French version of the terminologies while leveraging the manual original semantic integration effort made when the English version were included in the Metathesaurus.

The lack of anchorage of translated medical terminologies in the UMLS represents a real barrier for non-English-speaking communities that produce and manage biomedical data in their own languages. For example, France, Spain, Italy or Germany. UMLS concepts and semantic types are often used as gold standard annotations is most annotation tasks/campaigns for biomedical information extraction (e.g. some tasks of the CLEF eHealth evaluation campaign in 2015 and 2016 with the Quaero corpus (Névéol et al., 2014)).

To ensure semantic interoperability it is not enough to just translate ontologies, we must also formally keep the link between objects of the translated ontologies and the original one. Such data also needs to be semantically represented to be exploitable by machines (e.g., Linked Open Data vision). In previous work, we have reconciled more than 228K mappings between ten English ontologies hosted on NCBO BioPortal and their French translations hosted on the SIFR BioPortal. But still, the UMLS identifiers were missing. Re-establishing the broken links between English UMLS sources and their French counterpart, not included in the UMLS, was the aim of this work.

In the remainder of the paper, we first present background and related work about French medical terminologies and their relation to UMLS. Subsequently, we present the enrichment methodology and algorithm based on information extracted from class labels, multilingual translation mappings and codes. Then we evaluate the impact of the enrichment on the SIFR Annotator performance on the Quaero corpus, before concluding and giving some future perspectives.

2   Related Work

2.1   SIFR BioPortal

In the context of the Semantic Indexing of French Biomedical Data Resources (SIFR) project, we have developed the SIFR BioPortal (`http://BioPortal.lirmm.fr`) Jonquet et al. (2016), an open platform to host French biomedical ontologies and terminologies based on the technology developed by the US National Center for Biomedical Ontology (Noy et al., 2009; Whetzel and Team, 2013). The portal facilitates the use and fostering of ontologies by offering a set of services such as search and browsing, mapping hosting and generation, metadata edition, versioning, visualization, recommendation, community feedback, etc. As of today, the portal contains 24 public ontologies and terminologies (+ 6 private ones) that cover multiple areas of biomedicine, such as the French versions of MeSH, MedDRA, ATC, ICD-10, or WHO-ART but also multilingual ontologies (for which only the French content is parsed) such as Rare Human Disease Ontology, OntoPneumo or Ontology of Nuclear Toxicity. The SIFR BioPortal includes the SIFR Annotator[2] a publicly accessible and easily usable ontology-based annotation tool to process text data in French. This service is originally based on the NCBO Annotator (Jonquet et al., 2009), a web service allowing scientists to utilize available biomedical ontologies for annotating their datasets automatically, but was significantly enhanced and customized for French. The annotator service processes raw textual descriptions input by users, tags them with relevant biomedical ontology concepts and returns the annotations to the users in several formats such as JSON-LD, RDF or BRAT. A preliminary evaluation Jonquet et al. (2016) showed that the web service matches the results of previously reported work in French, while being public, functional and turned toward semantic web standards. SIFR

---

[2]`http://BioPortal.lirmm.fr/annotator`

Annotator allows users to input free text and to annotate the text with ontology concepts. SIFR Annotator, uses a dictionary composed of a flat list of terms build the concept labels and synonym labels from all the resources uploaded in SIFR BioPortal (ontologies, terminologies, vocabularies, dictionaries). SIFR BioPortal currently contains about 255K concepts and around twice that number of terms.

Enabling the service to use additional ontologies is as simple as uploading them to the portal (the indexing and dictionary generation are automatic).

2.2 Ontology Alignment and French Biomedical Ontologies

There have been initiatives in the past to reinforce the involvement of French language in the UMLS which contains now 5 French terminologies (Darmoni et al., 2003; Zweigenbaum et al., 2003; Annane et al., 2016). However, most of the French ontologies and terminologies are still not included; they are most often aggregated and translated by the CISMeF group[3] (Grosjean et al., 2011) (324.000 French concepts in HeTOP vs. 85,000 in the native UMLS) and since more recently also offered within the SIFR BioPortal (Jonquet et al., 2016).

There are very few attempts at aligning French biomedical terminologies/ontologies between each other or with equivalent English-language ontologies. The UMLS Metathesaurus itself can be considered as a large scale ontology alignment initiative, as it constitutes a pivot-based alignment of medical terminologies in several languages (Bodenreider et al., 1998). As for French-specific ontology translation and alignment, the work on MeSH by the French organization INSERM[4] is a good example. However, the most important effort in France is achieved by the Rouen University Hospital within the context of the CisMeF project (Merabti et al., 2012).

When integrating and translating new terminologies within the HeTOP platform(Grosjean et al., 2011) , they performed they generally aligned the new content with the UMLS. Although that information was poorly represented (e.g., CUIs were encoded as labels)s in the OWL version exported from HeTOP and imported into the SIFR BioPortal, we reused that information during our enrichment process. .

Previous work by Annane et al. (2016) explored the reconciliation of the French terminologies and ontologies in the SIFR BioPortal with their equivalent English ontologies within the NCBO BioPortal. Now, the locally hosted ontologies are formally aligned and the alignments are available within the SIFR BioPortal, adapted to allow interportal mappings. In most cases, the mappings were produced through a code reconciliation between the ontologies. We have used these multilingual translation mappings in the present work.

Even in English, there is little work related to enriching existing English-language biomedical ontologies with UMLS CUIs, let alone French-language ontologies.Rajput and Gurulingappa (2013) use direct concept name matching to establish a correspondence between UMLS and their own neurodegenerative disease ontology composed of 1147 concepts. Sarkar et al. (2003) apply a range of ontology matching techniques (exact-match, match on normalized UMLS strings and using MetaMap) to enrich the Gene Ontology (GO) with UMLS semantic information. There are, to our knowledge no attempts at enriching French biomedical ontologies and terminologies automatically with UMLS concepts and semantic types.

The UMLS group within the SIFR BioPortal contains 10 medical terminologies (Table 1). Three terminologies (highlighted in gray in Table 1) where directly extracted from the UMLS with a customized version of the NCBO developed umls2rdf tool (`https://github.com/sifrproject/umls2rdf`). For these three terminologies no enrichment was necessary, as the output generated by the tool already included UMLS CUIs and TUIs. The rest of the seven ontologies (highlighted in blue in Table 1) where generated by an OWL export from the HeTOP platform and although they English counterpart was included in the UMLS, the French version did not have CUI and TUI information.

---

[3]Rouens University Hospital (`http://www.chu-rouen.fr/cismef/`)

[4]`http://www.inserm.fr/`

3   Methods

4 of the 7 terminologies studied already contain most CUI and TUI information, but poorly encoded as a `skos:altLabel` among the numerous other labels of the classes. For the remaining ontologies, the information had to be found independently either through existing multilingual translation mappings or directly through querying UMLS Metathesaurus through its SQL interface. Our goal is to formally represent CUIs with the `umls:cui` property and TUIs with the `umls:tui` relation, where the `umls` namespace is defined as: `http://BioPortal.bioontology.org/ontologies/umls/`. By using this namespace, the NCBO and SIFR BioPortal can automatically recognize UMLS identifiers and use them properly within the platform services, especially when filtering annotations created by the Annotators. We applied the following algorithm for each class of the ontology (each subclass of `owl:Class`):

1. Query the existing ontology, retrieve all alternative labels and attempt to match a CUI of the form CXXXXXXX with a regular expression, where each X is a digit.

2. If no CUIs were defined as class labels, use multiligual mappings (Annane et al., 2016). If a mapping is found, query the corresponding English language version of the resource in the NCBO BioPortal and retrieve the CUIs.

3. If no mapping is found (or no CUI information), extract code (unique code in the source ontology) either directly through the `skos:notation` relation, when it is available or from parsing the URIs of the classes. Query UMLS through the UMLS SQL interface to retrieve the CUIs.

4. Otherwise, the class remains without CUIs.

Once we obtain all the CUIs for each class (when possible), we retrieve the corresponding semantic types for each CUIs through the UMLS SQL interface and add them to the model through the `umls:tui` property.

We implemented this algorithm in Java, using the Jena library to load the source and target ontologies as well as the mappings. We used the 2015ab version of UMLS loaded on a MySQL server that we accessed through the Java JDBC API. The algorithms were applied on the ontologies one-by-one. The implementation is available on github[5]. Table 1 quantifies the results of the CUI enrichment.

4   Evaluation

An interesting use-case for the enrichment of the French biomedical ontologies from SIFR BioPortal with UMLS CUIs is the evaluation of the named entity recognition performance of SIFR Annotator on the Quaero Annotated Corpus (Névéol et al., 2014).

The Quaero corpus is a French-language corpus in the biomedical domain for the evaluation of named entity recognition and normalization. Quaero is more specifically composed of two sub-corpora, EMEA which contains information on marketed drugs and the MEDLINE corpus,which contains titles from PubMed abstract titles. The annotations consist of token or phrase boundaries of identified entities, the corresponding UMLS semantic groups and one or more UMLS CUIs. A semantic group is a thematic grouping of several semantic types, for example "Disorder" or "Procedures". The 10 Semantic Groups are often used as coarse-grained groupings of UMLS Semantic Types (McCray et al., 2001).

The corpus was created by instructing bilingual annotators to annotate the French text with UMLS semantics groups and CUIs based on their English language descriptions and definitions as included in UMLS. This process actually biases the corpus, as there is an implicit translation task hidden within the evaluation of the named entity recognition, which creates a disadvantage for a system such as the SIFR BioPortal annotator that annotates directly with French biomedical ontologies rather than using a translation-based approach.

---

[5]`https://github.com/sifrproject/sifr_project_java_ontology_processing`

Ontology	#Classes	w/o CUI	w/o TUI	In label	In mapng.	Through code	#Remaining w/o CUI	#Remaining w/o TUI
CIF	1496	1496	1495	1495	0	0	1	1
CISP2	745	742	682	682	0	61	2	2
CIM-10	19853	19853	19813	12021	7792	0	40	40
MDRFRE	66382	4	66378	0	0	0	4	4
MSHFRE	27459	4	0	0	0	0	4	4
MTHMSTFRE	1704	4	1700	0	0	0	4	4
MEDLINEPLUS	849	849	795	795	0		54	54
SNMIFRE	106291	106291	102093	96756	5337	127	4071	4071
WHO-ARTFRE	3483	3483	3482	3320	162	0	1	1
ATCFRE	5768	5768	5755	0	0	5755	13	13

Table 1: Statistics for the ontologies enriched in CUIs (all UMLS ontologies with a French-language version): Number of classes, number of classes without CUIs at the beginning, the number of classes without CUIs at the beginning, the number of CUIs found in labels, the number of CUIs found through mappings, the number of CUIs found through UMLS codes, the number of classes remaining without CUIs at the end and the number of ontologies remaining without semantic types at the end.

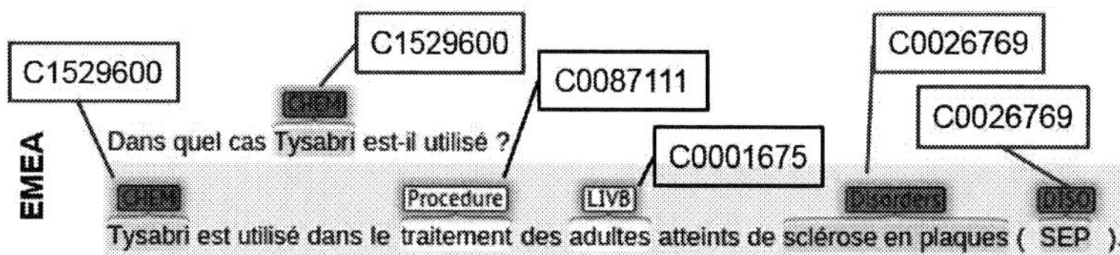

Figure 1: An illustration of the type of annotations in the Quaero corpus. From Névéol et al. 2014.

The evaluation of the named entity recognition is bound to the proper recognition of its semantic group: if the token boundaries (NER) or the CUI identified are correct but the semantic group is incorrect, the annotation is counted as incorrect. This is a confounding factor in the evaluation of NER alone, as the absence of semantic types in a particular ontology will lead to false negatives, although the entity was identified. Figure 1 illustrates the annotations expected in the Quaero corpus.

The SIFR Annotator proposes a specific output format for the Quaero evaluation and several variants. The `quaero` output is the direct output of the annotations as they are returned. The `quaerosg` format is the same, except that when there are several possible semantic groups, the first is chosen. The `quaeroimg` output excludes annotations with ambiguous semantic groups altogether. Although the interface does not show it, the formats can be used through the `format=quaero/quaeroimg/quaerosg` option of the REST API.

Corpus or System	NER + Semantic Groups			NER + Semantic Groups + CUIs		
	P (%)	R (%)	F1 (%)	P (%)	R (%)	F1 (%)
EMEA before	7.44	16.47	10.25	6.21	15.36	8.89
EMEA after	69.98	48.61	57.37	42.55	29.32	34.61
MEDLINE before	29.97	57.91	39.50	12.10	24.31	16.16
MEDLINE after	70.06	51.94	59.65	40.87	30.64	35.02

Table 2: The results on the Quaero corpus before and after the CUI enrichment.

We run the evaluation of the SIFR Annotator on the test sets of the EMEA and MEDLINE sub-corpora in Quaero with all the possible UMLS ontologies in SIFR BioPortal. Table 2 presents the compared results. Before the enrichment only MDRFRE, MSHFRE and MTHMSTFRE had CUI information, the lack of CUIs and semantic types prevented the proper annotation and led to very low precision and recall. The fact that the MEDLINE corpus has somewhat better results is due to its good coverage by the MSHFRE, MDREFRE and MTHMSTFRE ontologies. The CUI/TUI enrichment process allowed us to eliminate the precision/recall issue, however errors remain because of ambiguous annotations (a phrase or text generates several annotations where the corpus expects only one). We are now working on addressing these more specific issues with a word sense disambiguation component in SIFR Annotator.

The enrichment in semantic types and CUIs also enables to filtering of annotation results by semantic group with all of the French UMLS source ontologies (Figure 2).

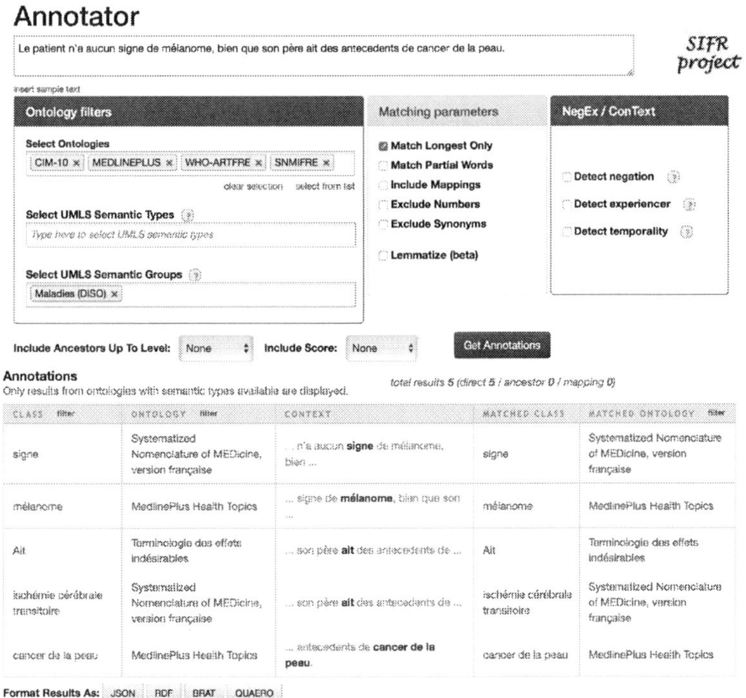

Figure 2: An example of annotation filtering with UMLS semantic types and groups in SIFR BioPortal Annotator.

5   Conclusions and Future Work

We have proposed an approach to enrich French biomedical ontologies in SIFR BioPortal with UMLS CUIs and semantic types in order to improve the annotation performance of SIFR annotator for UMLS based NER tasks. While we achieve our goal on the context of the evaluation on the Quaero corpus, the approach relied only existing mappings and a code interoperability between UMLS and its source ontologies, which is a good start, but does not allow to enrich arbitrary ontologies. The integration of multilingual ontology mapping algorithms into the process may make the small tool we developed for the alignment worthy of integration directly into SIFR BioPortal to allow on-the-fly enrichment whenever a user submits an ontology.

We have described a method to enrich French medical terminologies in the SIFR BioPortal with UMLS concepts and semantic type identifiers in order to improve the annotation performance of SIFR Annotator for UMLS based named entity recognition tasks. While we achieve our goal in the context of the evaluation on the Quaero corpus, the task was relatively easy, but fastidious, as we could rely on existing multilingual translation mappings and/or a code reconciliation between UMLS sources and the French translated terminologies. Our future perspective is to automatically enable such an enrichment (at least with TUIs) for any ontology uploaded to the SIFR BioPortal. We believe we could rely on knowledge-based ontology alignment techniques to achieve this result.

References

Annane, A., V. Emonet, F. Azouaou, and C. Jonquet (2016). Multilingual mapping reconciliation between english-french biomedical ontologies. In *6th International Conference on Web Intelligence, Mining and Semantics, WIMS'16*, Number 13, pp. 12. ACM.

Bodenreider, O. (2004, 01). The unified medical language system (umls): integrating biomedical terminology. *Nucleic Acids Research 32*(Database issue), D267–D270.

Bodenreider, O., S. J. Nelson, W. T. Hole, and H. F. Chang (1998). Beyond synonymy: exploiting the umls semantics in mapping vocabularies. pp. 815–819. American Medical Informatics Association.

Bollegala, D., G. Kontonatsios, and S. Ananiadou (2015, 06). A cross-lingual similarity measure for detecting biomedical term translations. *PLOS ONE 10*(6), 1–28.

Darmoni, S., E. Jarrousse, P. Zweigenbaum, P. Le Beux, F. Namer, R. Baud, M. Joubert, H. Vallée, R. Côté, A. Buemi, D. Bourigault, G. Recourcé, S. Jeanneau, and J. Rodrigues (2003). Vumef: Extending the french involvement in the umls metathesaurus. *AMIA Annual Symposium Proceedings 2003*, 824–824.

Grosjean, J., T. Merabti, N. Griffon, B. Dahamna, and S. Darmoni (2011, 8–10 November). Multiterminology cross-lingual model to create the european health terminology/ontology portal. In *Short papers of the 9th International Conference on Terminology and Artificial Intelligence, TIA 2011*, Paris, pp. 118–121.

Jonquet, C., A. Annane, K. Bouarech, V. Emonet, and S. Melzi (2016, July). SIFR BioPortal : Un portail ouvert et gnrique dontologies et de terminologies biomdicales franaises au service de lannotation smantique. In *16th Journes Francophones d'Informatique Mdicale, JFIM'16*, Genve, Suisse, pp. 16.

Jonquet, C., V. Emonet, and M. A. Musen (2015, June). Roadmap for a multilingual BioPortal. In *MSW4'15: 4th Workshop on the Multilingual Semantic Web*, Volume 1532 of *CEUR Workshop Proceedings*, Portoroz, Slovenia.

Jonquet, C., N. H. Shah, and M. A. Musen (2009, March). The Open Biomedical Annotator. In *American Medical Informatics Association Symposium on Translational BioInformatics, AMIA-TBI'09*, San Francisco, CA, USA, pp. 56–60.

McCray, A. T., A. Burgun, and O. Bodenreider (2001). Aggregating UMLS semantic types for reducing conceptual complexity. *Studies in health technology and informatics 84*(0 1), 216.

Merabti, T., L. F. Soualmia, J. Grosjean, M. Joubert, and S. J. Darmoni (2012). Aligning biomedical terminologies in french: Towards semantic interoperability in medical applications. In S. Mordechai and R. Sahu (Eds.), *Medical Informatics*, Engineering Technology in Medicine. InTech.

Néveol, A., C. Grouin, J. Leixa, S. Rosset, and P. Zweigenbaum (2014). The QUAERO French medical corpus: A ressource for medical entity recognition and normalization. In *Proc of BioTextMining Work*, pp. 24–30.

Noy, N. F., N. H. Shah, P. L. Whetzel, B. Dai, M. Dorf, N. B. Griffith, C. Jonquet, D. L. Rubin, M.-A. Storey, C. G. Chute, and M. A. Musen (2009, May). BioPortal: ontologies and integrated data resources at the click of a mouse. *Nucleic Acids Research 37*((web server)), 170–173.

Rajput, A. M. and H. Gurulingappa (2013). Semi-automatic approach for ontology enrichment using umls. *Procedia Computer Science 23*, 78 – 83. 4th International Conference on Computational Systems-Biology and Bioinformatics, CSBio2013.

Sarkar, I. N., M. N. Cantor, R. Gelman, F. Hartel, and Y. A. Lussier (2003). Linking biomedical language information and knowledge resources: Go and umls. *Pac Symp Biocomput*, 439–450.

Whetzel, P. L. and N. Team (2013, April). NCBO Technology: Powering semantically aware applications. *Biomedical Semantics 4S1*(S8), 49.

Zweigenbaum, P., R. Baud, A. Burgun, F. Namer, E. Jarrousse, N. Grabar, P. Ruch, F. Le Duff, B. Thirion, and S. Darmoni (2003). Towards a unified medical lexicon for french. *Stud Health Technol Inform 95*, 415–420.

Experiments in taxonomy induction in Spanish and French

Irene Renau
Pontificia Universidad
Católica de Valparaíso
`irene.renau@pucv.cl`

Rogelio Nazar
Pontificia Universidad
Católica de Valparaíso
`rogelio.nazar@pucv.cl`

Rafael Marín
Centre National de
la Recherche Scientifique
(Lille)
`rafael.marin@univ-lille3.fr`

Abstract

We present an ongoing project on taxonomy induction of nouns in Spanish and French. Experiments were first run in Spanish and, in this paper, we replicate the same method for French. Lexical taxonomies connect nouns following the IS-A structure: *árbol* ('tree') is a *planta* ('planta') is a *ser vivo* ('living being') is a *objeto físico* ('physical object'). In our proposal, we use a handmade shallow ontology of around 250 nodes and link every noun to one of these nodes. We use a set of algorithms based on corpus statistics techniques to build the hypernym-hyponym relations. As a result, any noun of Spanish or French can be linked to the taxonomy. Evaluation shows 60-90% precision, taking into account the best measures. At this stage of the process, our taxonomies can be already used for several NLP tasks such as semantic tagging of corpora, population of other taxonomies such as WordNet or applications in terminology. All the algorithms and a demo interface are available at `<http://www.tecling.com/kind>`.

1 Introduction

The present paper[1] describes a methodology for taxonomy induction in Spanish and French, using a combination of algorithms based on different quantitative approaches. At this stage of the project, we start with nouns because they are a central part-of-speech for conceptual categories. In our proposal, the major part of the algorithms receive raw corpus data as input, and as a result of all the process we obtain a taxonomic structure as output, linking each noun with its hypernym and building a hypernym chain. Previous results, as well as the algorithms used for the experiments and other material, are already published in `http://www.tecling.com`, a web page which is updated as we progress in the project.

From the lexical point of view, a taxonomy can be described as a structure of hypernymy relations, the so-called "IS A relations", e.g. *un martillo ES UNA herramienta ES UN artefacto ES UN objeto físico* ('a hammer IS A tool IS AN artifact IS a physical object'). Lexical taxonomies can contain other types of lexical relations such as synonymy or meronymy, as well as different parts-of-speech (verbs, nouns, adjectives, etc.). They are useful for a variety of tasks in natural language processing, as they organise raw linguistic data such as corpora. For example, they play an important role in corpus-based terminology and lexicography, as part of the process for automatising vocabulary extraction, creation of dictionaries, search for new terms, among other typical tasks in these areas.

Our approach in this project is mainly quantitative in order to facilitate the replication of the same experiments in different languages, as we do in the present paper for Spanish and French. Other languages will be included to the project as we progress.

[1]This paper received support of the Fondecyt Program (Conicyt, Chilean Government), Project nr. 11140704 and from Programa de Cooperación Científica Ecos-Conicyt, Project nr. C16H02.

We have been able to reduce the error rates of the procedure by using different algorithms combined, using a decision algorithm to decide via a voting system. Not all of the individual algorithms we use are new, but the novelty of the proposal lays on the way these algorithms are connected in a unified system.

In the following pages, we make a brief account of the state of the art in automatic taxonomy induction (section 2), we present our methodology (section 3), the results of the experiment conducted both for Spanish and French (section 4) and some conclusions and perspectives of future work (section 5).

2   Taxonomy induction: state of the art

There are countless ontologies or taxonomies used in a broad range of disciplines or professional areas, and the vast majority of these resources have been manually compiled by experts. For example, Cyc (Lenat, 1995) is an ontology for the general knowledge used for a variety of tasks in artificial intelligence; WordNet (Miller, 1995) and EuroWordNet (Vossen, 2004) are well-known taxonomies originally built by psychologists and linguists and widely used in natural language processing; and the CPA Ontology (Hanks, 2017a) is a shallow ontology used for semantic annotation of corpus data in a lexicographic project, the *Pattern Dictionary of English Verbs*, PDEV (Hanks, 2017b).

Manual resources have high precision, but they deal with different problems as well, the most important of them being how to update the resource without counting with a large team of trained experts working constantly on it. Initiatives such as the Observatory of Neology show that one can find new words and meanings almost in any copy of a newspaper, and that lexical and semantic change is the natural state of vocabulary. The same could be said about terminology, using scientific papers as source of information. For that reason, computational linguistics has been interested in the problem of taxonomy induction for decades.

First methods, conducted during the 70s and 80s, used computer-based dictionaries sources of taxonomic relations between the *definiendum* or hyponym and the *definiens* or hypernym. Hyernymy relations were extracted from dictionaries with rule-based methods (Calzolari, 1977; Amsler, 1981; Chodorow et al., 1985; Alshawi, 1989; Fox et al., 1988; Guthrie et al., 1990, among others). The advantage of these proposals was that they used reliable sources which can be considered already partially structured, as dictionaries work as "implicit taxonomies". However, these methods inherited the problems of lexicographic material, especially regarding the updating of the data but also in relation to the reliability of the data, because many dictionaries are not corpus-based even today.

Hearst (1992) proposed another strategy based on corpus linguistics, consisting of extracting definitional patterns from texts. For example, in a context such as "apples and other types of fruit", the pattern is "X and other types of Y", being X the hyponym and Y the hypernym. The strategy has been used in many studies (Rydin, 2002; Snow et al., 2006; Potrich and Pianta, 2008; Auger and Barrière, 2008; Aussenac-Gilles and Jacques, 2008, among others). This method is based on real data and facilitates the updating of information. However, it depends on a large amount of definitional rules, manually detected and compiled. Furthermore, these rules are language-dependent, which adds a difficulty to multilingual resources and in terms of replicability.

A third strategy consists of applying quantitative methods to taxonomy induction. Two main views can be outlined: on the one hand, many studies have shown interest in finding co-hyponym relations; that is, groups of words that are defined with the same hypernym, e.g. types of fruit, cheese, arms, emotions... (Grefenstette, 1994; Schütze and Pedersen, 1997; Lin, 1998; Alfonseca and Manandhar, 2002; Bullinaria, 2008). These words are said to be paradigmaticaly related, meaning that they tend to occur in similar syntagmatic contexts. Therefore, they are expected to share semantic features.

Another strategy consists of connecting hypernyms with their hyponyms through their asymmetric relationship when finding them in corpus: e.g. in a hypernym-hyponym pair such as *herramienta-martillo* ('tool-hammer'), it is more likely that *martillo* will appear in sentences with *herramienta* than vice versa, because *herramienta* can be used with other co-hyponyms of *martillo* such as *destornillador, llave, alicates* ('screwdriver, wrench, pliers'), etc. (Nazar et al., 2012). Also, as we do in this paper, Santus et al. (2014) also connect both tasks to create hypernymy chains using a combination of measures based on distributional semantics. Quantitative methods have the lack of precision as a potential problem, but the lack of certainty is compensated by the large amount of linguistic data. For that reason, this approach has become more popular and competitive since larger corpora have been available. Furthermore, being language-independent, they can be easily replicated and used to create multilingual resources.

3   Methodology

The methodology used for our experiments used the two quantitative approaches that were described in the previous section, combined. The general strategy consists of using an already created shallow ontology to build the top nodes of the taxonomy, which will be populated with the hypernymy chains, the latter step being the central part of the procedure. Spanish nouns are connected between them and also to the ontology nodes, building a hierarchical structure that includes the major part of the Spanish nouns, and any new noun can be processed and included in the taxonomy. The same procedure is applied to French. Both Spanish and French taxonomies are not connected at this stage of the project, but that is a task we are preparing for future work.

3.1   Materials

We used the CPA Ontology (Hanks, 2017a) to build the top nodes of the taxonomy. CPA Ontology is a shallow ontology of around 250 very general semantic types such as [[Process]], [[Action]], [[Physical Object]], etc. They do not include specialised information and many of them can be considered semantic primes (Wierzbicka, 1996), that is, concepts that cannot be defined with other concepts. For that reason, we consider the CPA Ontology as valid for any European language despite being originally created for English. Conversely, it would be not appropriate to use it when working with languages connected with very different cultures, such as the American indigenous languages or others.

Following the logic of using the CPA Ontology for the top nodes and leaving the automatic part for the most specific words, in our system the connection *roble > árbol > planta* ('oak > tree > plant') is automatic, but the connection *planta > objeto físico > entidad >* ('plant > physical object > entity') is part of the CPA Ontology. This way, most of the links have to be created automatically, but not in the case of the most general ones. Of course, the population of this shallow ontology (the process of connecting the nouns to the CPA's semantic types) is also automatic. This connection is triggered when a hypernym candidate is formally identical to some CPA semantic type.

The CPA is used only as a basic structure –it contains only 250 nodes which can be easily and even automatically translated to other languages. It has to be clarified as well that we can use any other ontology or taxonomy for the same purpose, and even the methodology can be applied to populate already existing resources such as WordNet. For example, we are starting to work with specialised vocabulary of Psychiatry, and for that purpose we are using a different ontology, also very general and with only 50 basic nodes.

Concerning the corpora, for algorithm 1 we used a lexicographic corpus which was necessary for one of the steps of the methodology. This corpus, consisting of noun definitions taken from online dictionaries, is a text file that has, in each row, nouns next to their definitions and, separated by a tab, different definitions for the same noun[2]. These definitions are used as plain text corpus, without metadata. For the algorithms 2 and 3, we used plain text extracted from Wikipedia, around 900 million words, without metadata or any kind of tagging. We used this corpus because it is big and open access, but the same method can be applied to any corpus with a similar or a larger size.

---

[2]We are preparing a different paper in which we explain our method to acquire, for any input noun, a set of definitions from the web.

3.2 Methods

3.2.1 Algorithm 1: analysis of *definiens-definiendum* co-occurrence

This algorithm analyses the lexicographic corpus to find hypernym-hyponym connections. Lexicographic entries are treated as plain text and all the text of the entries of all dictionaries sharing the same headword are grouped together in a sub-corpus, e.g. we group all the dictionary entries of *martillo* ('hammer'), obtaining a small set of raw text containing all the definitions of the different meanings of the word and even noisy information such as grammatical notes, etymology or abbreviations. The algorithm counts the number of times that a noun (the hypernym) co-occurs with nouns in the definitions (hypernym candidates). We assume that the noun which is more frequently used in the definitions of the different dictionaries in a specific entry is the hypernym, or hypernyms if the word is polysemous. For example, most of the dictionaries define *martillo* as *herramienta* ('tool'), which allows to create an IS A structure such as *martillo ES UNA herramienta* ('a hammer IS A tool').

The algorithm creates a list of candidates that correspond with the meaning(s) of the noun, eg. *herramienta, hueso, pieza, persona* ('tool, bone, piece, person'), etc. After the application of the rest of the algorithms, the results are confirmed or dismissed.

3.2.2 Algorithm 2: analysis of the asymmetric syntagmatic association

This algorithm uses the Wikipedia corpus to calculate the number of times that a target noun co-occurs with other nouns, then it calculates the number of times that one of these nouns co-occurs with the former noun. Based on the idea of asymmetric association between the hypernym and the hyponym, it is postulated that the hyponym tends to appear in the same sentences as its hypernym, but not the the other way around. We calculated these relations with directed charts that represent the co-occurrence relations of each word, in first and second degree. Figure 1 shows a graph representing these asymmetric relations found in corpus.

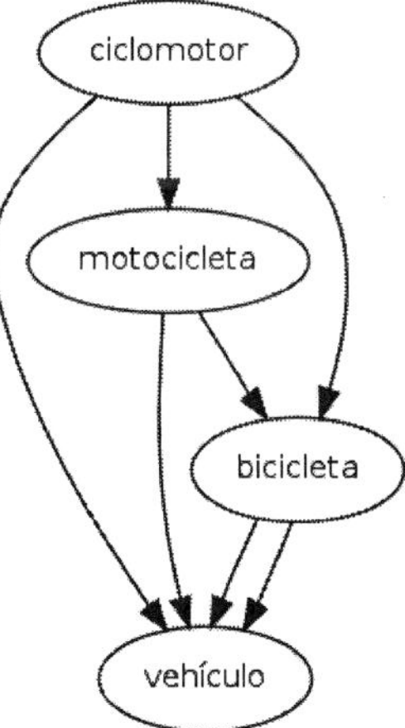

Figure 1: Example of a co-occurrence graph depicting the asymmetric relations between *ciclomotor* ('mopped') and its correct hypernym *vehículo* ('vehicle').

As observed in the graph, for the term *ciclomotor* ('moped'), the first-degree analysis points that it co-occurs with *motocicleta* ('motorbike') and *bicicleta* ('bicycle'). From this new analysis, we can observe that these two words appear in the same contexts that *vehículo* ('vehicle'), but this last term does not appear next to *ciclomotor, motocicleta* or *bicicleta*. These asymmetric relations are the ones considered hypernym clues. As a consequence, it can be concluded that "*ciclomotor* is a type of *vehículo*", simply because in this graph this is the node with the largest number of incoming arrows.

As in the case of the algorithm 1, here we also obtain hypernymy relations, in this case using a general corpus and with a different strategy. This pair of algorithms are necessary to build the taxonomical structure.

3.2.3 Algorithm 3: calculation of distributional similarity

As the algorithm 2, this algorithm also uses the Wikipedia corpus, but in this case to group different nouns sharing the same semantic type according to their distributional similarity. For example, the lexical items that refer to types of drinks, such as *café, vino, cerveza, té* ('coffee, wine, beer, tea', etc.) will show a tendency to appear in the same sentences with the same group of other units, such as *vaso, botella, beber*, (glass, bottle, drink, etc.). Therefore, for *café* there are bigrams such as *mucho café* ('a lot of coffee'), *buen café* ('good coffee'), *café ardiente* ('very hot coffee'), *café robusta* ('robusta coffee'), *tomar café* ('drink coffee'), etc. Each analysed word is associated with the lexical items co-occurring with it, and this association is represented as a word-vector, e.g. *café = {mucho, buen, ardiente, robusta, tomar...}*.

Once all analysed words are represented as vectors, the algorithm compares all of them against each other applying a similarity measure –the Jaccard coefficient– which calculates the degree of overlapping between vectors. As a result, we obtain groups of co-hyponyms, that is, words that can be defined with the same noun. This content is used to populate the labels that we previously obtain with algorithms 1 and 2. For example, if these algorithms established that *café* 'coffee' is a type of *bebida* 'drink', then every co-hyponym of *café* (such as *vino, cerveza, té...* in the previous example) will also be a type of 'drink'.

3.2.4 Algorithm 4: calculation of lexical and morphological similarity

This algorithm learns from the association between the lexical and formal features of the words with the conceptual categories they belong to. Unlike the previous algorithms, this particular one is not corpus-based. Instead, it only uses formal, non-linguistic information (such as components of the word defined as sequences of up to five letters at the beginning or end of each word). This way, if the system finds a lexical unit which cannot be found in corpus or if it is too infrequent to be analysed with the previous algorithms, then it will attempt to categorise whit unit using these formal features, in a process we term "analogical inference", because it learns from the categorisations conducted by the other algorithms.

In the lexical level, for example, it is possible to assume that if the previous algorithms have classified words such as *enfermedad celíaca* ('celiac disease') or *enfermedad pulmonar* ('lung disease') as hyponyms of *enfermedad* ('disease'), then via this analogical inference algorithm our system will classify a rarely used term such as *enfermedad de Knights* ('Knights' disease') as *enfermedad*. Also in the case of infrequent words such as *diverticulitis* ('diverticulitis'), the algorithm is able to infer that this word belong to the same group as other more frequent words, such as *apendicitis, laringitis* or *meningitis* ('appendicitis, laryngitis, meningitis'), because they share the same ending. This algorithm provides more flexibility and power of generalization to the system, since it implies a learning process that is conducted simultaneously to the analysis.

3.2.5 Algorithm 5: integration of methods

This final algorithm is in charge of the task of combining the information produced previous ones. Some of the previous algorithms collaborate and others reinforce the tasks already conducted. This integration is organised by a weighted voting procedure, considering the output generated by each of the algorithms presented above. It is weighted because algorithm 2 has twice the weight in this decision. In the event that a target word is found as a hyponym of both a direct parent and a grandparent, then the only criterion to decide between the two is the one that has been more frequently voted by the algorithms.

Furthermore, each decision will have attached a degree of certainty. For instance, if for an input noun there are more than two algorithms that coincide in placing such noun under a certain category, then the hypernymy link is presented with a high degree of certainty. If, instead, only two algorithms coincide in this, then such link only has a low degree of certainty. If only one algorithm is proposing this link, the proposal is ignored.

4   Results and evaluation

Results are shown as a list of candidates, each one taking the form of a hypernymy chain. The following is an example of such chains:

árbol > planta > entidad > todo

Here, the target word is the Spanish noun *árbol* ('tree'), which is automatically linked to its hypernym *planta* ('plant'). Then, the rest of the links (*planta > entidad > todo* 'plant > entity > everything') belong to the original structure of the CPA Ontology. Figures 2 and 3 show a graphic representation of the hypernymy chains for Spanish and French respectively.

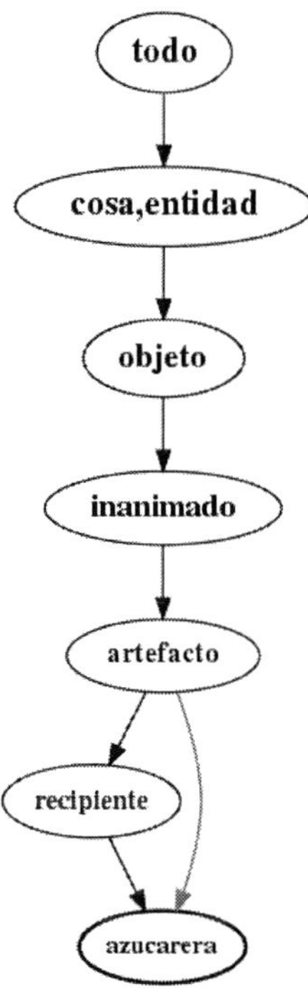

Figure 2: Result for Spanish noun *azucarera* ('sugar bowl')

In the example of figure 2, *azucarera* ('sugar bowl') is automatically linked to *recipiente* ('container') and *artefacto* ('artifact'), both semantic types of the CPA Ontology such as the rest of the nodes over them. Both links are correct, with different levels of semantic specification. In figure 3, the French word *bicyclette* ('bike') is also correctly linked to *véhicule roulant* ('vehicle with weels') and *véhicule* ('vehicle'), but the link to *roue* ('weel') is incorrect (it is actually a meronym). There are other correct and incorrect links in the structure shown in the figure, which is only a part of the whole net, e.g. the hyponyms linked to *bicyclette* are correct in the case of *ciclo-taxi* ('cycle taxi') but incorrect in the rest of the cases.

Regarding evaluation, we made a random sample of 100 nouns for each language and manually checked if the algorithm assigned hypernyms for each of them correctly. The sample is not stratified by frequency, which is detrimental for performance as most of the randomly selected words are infrequent. However, we leave for future work the development of an improved evaluation method.

Both for Spanish and French, criteria for precision consisted of considering as correct only those results with links that corresponded to a hypernym-hyponym relation, that is, when the target word could

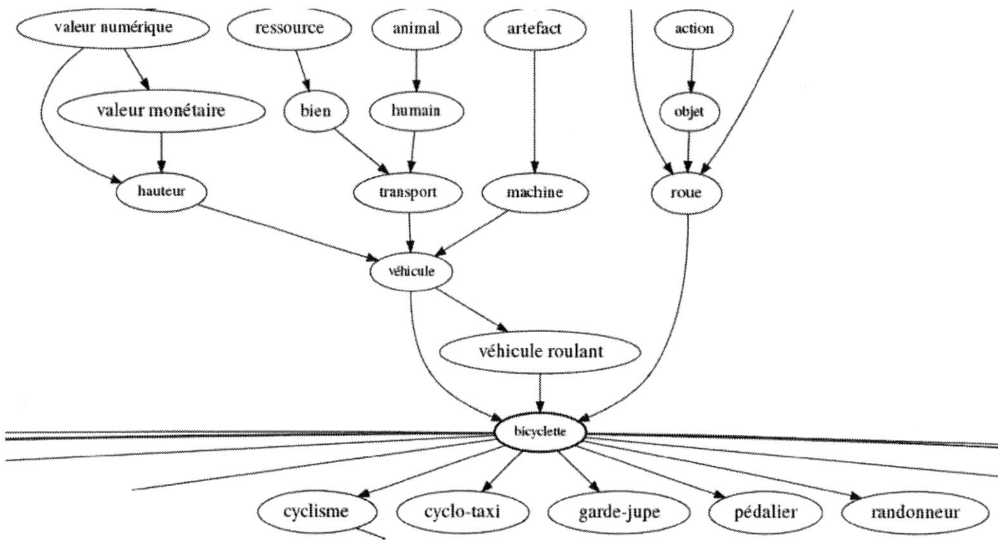

Figure 3: Result for French noun *bicyclette* (bike)

Table 1: Percentages of precision in the two languages by degree of certainty and rank of the candidate.

Rank	French		Spanish	
	High certainty	**All**	**High certainty**	**All**
1	60	51	54	46
2	76	65	74	65
3	83	70	78	68
4	90	74	78	71

be correctly linked to the upper node with the expression. In other words, we say there is a hypernym link between nouns X and Y if we can hold a statement such as "X is a type of Y", as in a "*bicyclette* is a type of *véhicule*". The rest of cases were considered incorrect. For instance, we marked as incorrect results such as "*termosifón* ('thermosyphon') is a type of *temperature* ('temperature')" for Spanish, or "*instructeur* ('instructor') is a type of *instruction* ('instruction')" for French. At this stage of our project, we did not calculate recall. Recall could in principle be defined as the number of senses detected per word over the total number of senses that actually exist for such word. We observed, however, that in the majority of the cases the system was only able to detect the most frequent meanings.

Precision was evaluated taking into account each position of the ranking and the degree of certainty of the algorithm. The rank of a candidate is given by the integration voting algorithm, thus the best candidate will be in the first position of the rank. We only considered the first 4 positions in ranking. Table 1 shows the intersection of results indicating high probability of success in each ranking position. If we only consider results ranked in the first position and with high degree of certainty, we obtain 60% precision in the French taxonomy and a 54% in the Spanish taxonomy. If we ignore the certainty level, results in first position drop to to 51% in French and a 46% in Spanish. Percentages of precision increase as we consider more positions in the ranking because then the system has more opportunities to find a correct hypernym.

The error analysis indicates that the major part of the errors are cases of semantic relations other than hypernymy. Typically, we found meronymy relations but also synonymy, co-hyponymy and even hyponymy. For example, in Spanish, the relation *aposento > edificio* ('chamber > building') corresponds to meronymy (*aposento* IS A PART OF *edificio*), and the same happens in French with *glacière > eau* ('glacier > water'). Also in the case of French, for the noun *produit* ('product'), one of the candidates for hypernym is actually a hyponym: *oeuvre d'art* ('piece of work'). Also incorrect is a result such as *copa > vaso* ('cup > glass') for Spanish, because the target word and the candidate are co-hyponyms.

Some of the errors are also due to interferences with the lexicographical marks coming from algorithm 1, such as in the case of the Spanish noun *pubis* ('pubis'), for which the candidate is *plural* ('plural'), due to the fact that many dictionaries indicate that the plural of this word is irregular. Problems regarding more general aspects of the methodology are related to the fact that the system does not distinguish between different candidates and different meanings at this stage of the project. Thus, for example, for a Spanish noun such as *taza* ('cup'), the system offers 4 candidates: *artefacto, vasija, recipiente* and *leche* ('artifact, vessel, vessel' and 'milk'). The first three candidates are correct, but they belong to the same meaning of the word, that is, all of them could be considered equivalent hypernyms. In the case of *artefacto*, the hypernym is the most general one, but it is correct because a cup is a type of physical object created by humans. The other two correct candidates are synonyms and, thus, equivalent and correct hypernyms, being *vasija* the old-fashion word and *recipiente* the modern one. Working on improving all these problems is part of our future work with the taxonomy project.

5   Conclusions and future work

In this paper, we have explained a methodology for creating a taxonomy based on a series of algorithms using different statistical approaches. Results shown in the previous section allow us to observe the advantages of the methodology, which connects a large number of vocabulary units via a corpus-driven analysis. The percentages of precision are still in need of improvement, but they are good enough to use the taxonomy for corpus semantic tagging and other NLP tasks. Renau and Nazar (2017), for instance, used these algorithm to tag arguments in order to study the semantics of verbs.

There are still a number of problems to be addressed in future work. For example, we are already testing the same method for specialised vocabulary, using a terminological ontology instead of the CPA Ontology, which was created for the analysis of general vocabulary. We are now working on different options to address the problems of polysemy, which are also an important source of problems in our taxonomy. In general, a more precise work is needed regarding evaluation and error analysis.

Another problem left for future work is to develop some strategy for the cases when a target word is found as a hyponym of both a direct parent and a grandparent. Now we only use the voting criterion, but a more sophisticated solution should be found, as some sort of reasoner which would be able to detect that both competing hypernyms are themselves a hyponym-hypernym pair. Similarly, the creation of a multilingual resource which could line up the taxonomies of Spanish, French and possibly other languages created independently is also left for future work. This alignment would be made by the extraction of bilingual vocabularies using parallel and comparable corpora.

References

Alfonseca, E. and S. Manandhar (2002). Extending a lexical ontology by a combination of distributional semantics signatures. In *International Conference on Knowledge Engineering and Knowledge Management*, pp. 1–7. Springer.

Alshawi, H. (1989). Computational lexicography for natural language processing. Chapter Analysing the Dictionary Definitions, pp. 153–69. White Plains, NY: Longman Publishing Group.

Amsler, R. A. (1981). A taxonomy for english nouns and verbs. In *Proceedings of the 19th annual meeting on Association for Computational Linguistics*, pp. 133–38. Association for Computational Linguistics.

Auger, A. and C. Barrière (2008). Pattern-based approaches to semantic relation extraction special issue of terminology. *Terminology 14*(1), 1–19.

Aussenac-Gilles, N. and M.-P. Jacques (2008). Designing and evaluating patterns for relation acquisition from texts with caméléon. *Terminology 14*(1), 45–73.

Bullinaria, J. A. (2008). Semantic categorization using simple word co-occurrence statistics. In *Proceedings of the ESSLLI Workshop on Distributional Lexical Semantics*, pp. 1–8.

Calzolari, N. (1977). An empirical approach to circularity in dictionary definitions. *Cahiers de Lexicologie Paris 31*(2), 118–28.

Chodorow, M. S., R. J. Byrd, and G. E. Heidorn (1985). Extracting semantic hierarchies from a large on-line dictionary. In *Proceedings of the 23rd annual meeting on Association for Computational Linguistics*, pp. 299–304. Association for Computational Linguistics.

Fox, E. A., J. T. Nutter, T. Ahlswede, M. Evens, and J. Markowitz (1988). Building a large thesaurus for information retrieval. In *Proceedings of the Second Conference on Applied Natural Language Processing*, pp. 101–8. Association for Computational Linguistics.

Grefenstette, G. (1994). *Explorations in Automatic Thesaurus Discovery*. Norwell, MA, USA: Kluwer Academic Publishers.

Guthrie, L., B. Slator, Y. Wilks, and R. Bruce (1990). Is there content in empty heads? In *Proc. of the 13th International Conference on Computational Linguistics, COLING'90 (Helsinki, Finland)*, pp. 138–143.

Hanks, P. (2017a). CPA ontology. http://www.pdev.org.uk/#onto. [last access: 31/8/2017].

Hanks, P. (2017b). Pattern dictionary of english verbs. http://www.pdev.org.uk/. [last access: 31/8/2017].

Hearst, M. A. (1992). Automatic acquisition of hyponyms from large text corpora. In *Proceedings of the 14th conference on Computational linguistics-Volume 2*, pp. 539–45. Association for Computational Linguistics.

Lenat, D. (1995). Cyc: a large-scale investment in knowledge infrastructure. *Communications of the ACM 38*(11), 33–38.

Lin, D. (1998). Automatic retrieval and clustering of similar words. In *Proceedings of the 17th International Conference on Computational linguistics-Volume 2*, pp. 768–74. Association for Computational Linguistics.

Miller, G. A. (1995). WordNet: A Lexical Database for English. *Communications of the ACM 38*(11), 39–41.

Nazar, R., J. Vivaldi, and L. Wanner (2012). Co-occurrence graphs applied to taxonomy extraction in scientific and technical corpora. *Procesamiento del Lenguaje Natural 49*, 67–74.

Potrich, A. and E. Pianta (2008, May). L-isa: Learning domain specific isa-relations from the web. In *Proceedings of the Sixth International Language Resources and Evaluation Conference (LREC 2008)*.

Renau, I. and R. Nazar (2017). Verbos in contexto: una propuesta para la detección automática de patrones léxicos en corpus. In I. Sariego López, J. G. Cuadrado, and C. G. Escribano (Eds.), *El diccionario en la encrucijada: de la sintaxis y la cultura al desafío digital*, pp. 879– 897. Santander: AELEX.

Rydin, S. (2002, July). Building a hyponymy lexicon with hierarchical structure. In *Proceedings of the ACL-02 Workshop on Unsupervised Lexical Acquisition*, Philadelphia, Pennsylvania, USA, pp. 26–33. Association for Computational Linguistics.

Santus, E., A. Lenci, Q. Lu, and S. Shulte im Walde (2014). Chasing hypernyms in vector spaces with entropy. In *Proceedings of the 14th Conference of the European Chapter of the Association for Computational Linguistics*, pp. 38–42.

Schütze, H. and J. O. Pedersen (1997, May). A cooccurrence-based thesaurus and two applications to information retrieval. *Information Processing and Management 33*(3), 307–18.

Snow, R., D. Jurafsky, and A. Y. Ng (2006). Semantic taxonomy induction from heterogenous evidence. In *Proceedings of the 21st International Conference on Computational Linguistics and the 44th annual meeting of the Association for Computational Linguistics*, pp. 801–8. Association for Computational Linguistics.

Vossen, P. (2004). Eurowordnet: a multilingual database of autonomous and language-specific wordnets connected via an inter-lingual index. *International Journal of Lexicography 17*(2), 161–173.

Wierzbicka, A. (1996). *Semantics: Primes and Universals*. Oxford: Oxford University Press.

A statistical model for morphology inspired by the Amis language

Isabelle Bril[*]
Lacito-CNRS
Isabelle.Bril@cnrs.fr

Achraf Lassoued
University Paris II
achraflassoued985@gmail.com

Michel de Rougemont
University of Paris II, IRIF-CNRS
mdr@irif.fr

Abstract

We introduce a statistical model for the morphology of natural languages. As words contain a root and potentially a prefix and a suffix, we associate three vector components, one for the root, one for the prefix, and one for the suffix. As the morphology captures important semantic notions and syntactic instructions, a new *Content vector c* can be associated with the sentences. It can be computed online and used to find the most likely derivation tree in a grammar. The model was inspired by the analysis of *Amis*, an Austronesian language with a rich morphology.

1 Introduction

The representation of words as vectors of small dimension, introduced by the Word2vec system Mikolov et al. (2013), is based on the correlation of occurrences of two words in the same sentence, or the second moment of the distribution of words[1]. It is classically applied to predict a missing word in a sentence or to detect an odd word in a list of words. Computational linguists Socher et al. (2013) also studied how to extend the vector representation of the words to a vector representation of the sentences, capturing some key semantic parameters such as Tense, Voice, Mood, Illocutionary force and Information structure.

Words have an internal structure, also called morphology. The word *preexisting*, for example, has a prefix *pre-*, a root *exist* and a suffix *-ing*. In this case, we write *pre-exist-ing* to distinguish these three components. Given some texts, we can then analyse the most frequent prefixes, the distribution of prefix occurrences, the distribution of suffixes given a root, and so on. We call these statistical distributions the *Morphology Statistics* of the language.

In this paper, we consider the second moment of the *Morphology Statistics* and can determine which prefix is the most likely in a missing word of a sentence, which suffix is unlikely given a prefix and a sentence, and many other predictions. We argue that these informations are very useful to associate a vector representation to sentences and therefore to capture some key semantic and syntactic parameters. As an example, we selected *Amis*, a natural language with profuse morphology which is well suited for this analysis. *Amis* is one of the twenty-four Austronesian languages originally spoken in Taiwan, only fifteen of which are still spoken nowadays. This approach can be applied to any other language.

Amis belongs to the putative Eastern Formosan subgroup of the great Austronesian family Blust (1999); Sagart (2004); Ross (2009). *Amis* is spoken along the eastern coast of Taiwan and has four main dialects which display significant differences in their phonology, lexicon and morphosyntactic properties. The analysis bears

---

[*]This research is financed by the "Typology and dynamics of linguistic systems" strand of the Labex EFL (Empirical Foundations of Linguistics) (ANR-10-LABX-0083/CGI).

[1]The third moment is the distribution of triples of words and the k-th moment is the distribution of k words.

on Northern Amis; the data were collected during fieldwork. A prior study of the northern dialect Chen (1987) dealt mostly with verbal classification and the voice system.

We built a tool to represent the statistical morphology of *Amis*, given a set of texts where each word has been decomposed into components (i.e. prefix, infix, root and suffix). The tool is similar to the OLAP (Online Analytical Processing) Analysis used for Data Analysis.

- We can analyse the global distribution of prefixes, roots, suffixes, i.e. the most frequent occurrences.

- Given a root (or a prefix, or a suffix), we obtain the distribution of the pairs (Prefixes;Suffixes) of that root, and the distribution of the prefixes, or the distribution of the suffixes by projection. Similarly for a given prefix, or a given suffix.

We then study the second moment of the *Morphology Statistics* and are able to predict the most likely prefix, root or suffix given a sequence of words. As some prefixes or suffixes carry some semantic and syntactic information, as it is the case in *Amis*, we build a *Content* vector for a sentence, and then predict the parsing of a sentence. Our results are:

- A statistical representation of prefixes, roots and suffixes, as structured vectors,

- A vector representation for a sentence, the *Content vector*. We show its use to predict the most likely derivation tree.

In the next section, we introduce the basic concepts. In the third section, we present our statistical model to capture the morphology of a natural language and apply it to *Amis*. In the fourth section, we describe its use for a syntactic and semantic analysis.

2   Preliminaries

We review some basic statistics in the context of natural languages in section 2.1 and the *Amis* language in section 2.2.

2.1   Basic Statistics

Let $s = w_1.w_2...w_n$ be a sentence with the words w_i on some alphabet Σ. Let ustat(s) be the *uniform statistics*, also called the 1-gram vector of the sentence s. It is a vector whose dimension is the size of the dictionary, the number of distinct words. The value ustat$(s)[w]$ is $\#w$ the number of occurrences of w divided by n, the total number of occurrences.

$$\text{ustat}(s) = \frac{1}{n} . \begin{pmatrix} \#w_1 \\ \#w_2 \\ ... \\ \#w_m \end{pmatrix}$$

We can also interpret ustat(s) as the distribution over the words w_i observed on a random position in a text. When the context is clear, we may also display the absolute values as opposed to the relative values of the distribution. Variations of these distributions are used in Computational Linguistics Manning and Schütze (1999); Baayen (2008).

Suppose we take two random positions i, j and define the ustat$^2(s)$ vector as the density of the pairs (w_i, w_j). It would be the second moment of the distribution of the words. For simplicity, we consider the symmetric covariance matrix $M(w_i, w_j)$ which gives the number of occurrences of the pair (w_i, w_j), i.e. without order. One can view the covariance matrix as the probability to observe a pair of words in a sentence and the diagonal values of the matrix give the first moment.

Given a (n, n) covariance matrix, one can associate a vector of v_i dimension n to each w_i such that the dot product $v_i.v_j$ is equal to $M(w_i, w_j)$. If we only select the large eigenvalues of M, we can obtain vectors of smaller dimension such that $w_i.w_j \simeq M(w_i, w_j)$. This PCA (Principal Component Analysis) method goes back to the 1960s, uses the SVD (Singular Value) Decomposition of the (n, n) matrix and has an $O(n^3)$ time complexity. In Mikolov et al. (2013), a learning technique is used to obtain vectors of dimension 200 when the dictionary has $n = 10^4$ words. In this paper, we refine this approach by separating the covariance matrices of prefixes, roots and suffixes. As we observe 30 distinct prefixes and 10 distinct suffixes, a direct SVD decomposition is efficient.

2.2 The Amis language

A fundamental property of Amis is that roots[2] are most generally underspecified and categorially neutral Bril (2017); they are fully categorised (as nouns, verbs, modifiers, etc.) after being derived and inflected as morphosyntactic word forms and projected in a clause.

Primary derivation operates on roots and is basically category attributing; it derives noun stems and verb stems. Noun stems are flagged by the noun marker *u* or by demonstratives. Verb stems display voice affixes, Actor Voice *mi-* (AV), Undergoer Voice *ma-* (UV), passive voice *-en*, Locative *-an*.

Secondary derivation occurs on primarily derived verb stems: (i) operating category-changing derivation (i.e. deverbal nouns, modifiers, etc.). (ii) deriving applicative voices[3] (Instrumental *sa-*, and Conveyance *si-*). For instance, *mi-* stems are derived as instrumental *sa-pi-* forms, *ma-* stems are derived as instrumental *sa-ka-* forms.

Some other brief indications (see section 4.4 for further details), nouns are case-marked; voice-affixed verbs select a nominative pivot/subject with the same semantic role.

3 A statistical model for morphology

We first built a tool *Morphix* which, given several texts, constructs the distribution of prefixes, suffixes and roots. Given a root, we can display the distribution of its affixes. Similarly, we can give a prefix (resp. a suffix) and represent the distribution of roots and suffixes (resp. prefixes). We then consider the second moment distributions of prefixes, suffixes and roots. We build their vector representations. If we combine them, we obtain a structured decomposition of the original words.

3.1 Basic Statistics for the Amis language

The distribution of all prefixes and suffixes, given 70 Amis texts with more than 4000 words, is given in Figure 1. All the charts use absolute values. The *Morphix* tool provides an interface where a root (resp. a prefix or a suffix) can be selected and the distribution of prefixes and suffixes for a given root are graphically displayed, as in Figure 2.

---

[2] A *root* is an atomic word without affixes. Affixes are either inflectional (i.e. express a semantic or syntactic function), or derivational (i.e. create different categories.

[3] With applicative voices, the promoted non-core term (i.e. locative, instrumental, conveyed entity) becomes the nominative pivot of the derived verb form, with the same syntactic alignment as Undergoer Voice.

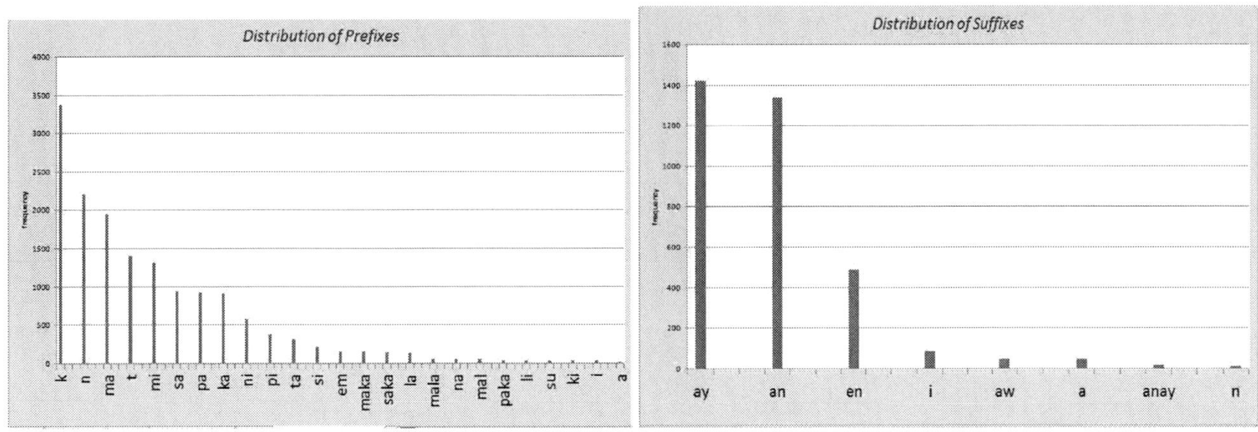

Figure 1: Most frequent prefixes and suffixes.

Given the distribution of (prefixes;suffixes)[4] of Figure 2, we obtain by projection the distribution of prefixes and suffixes in Figure 3 for this specific root.

3.2   Vector representation of prefixes, roots and suffixes

Given a (n, n) correlation matrix M, the SVD (Singular Value decomposition), produces n vectors v_i of dimension n such that $v_i.v_j = M(v_i, v_j)$. If we project v_i on the large eigenvalues of M, we reduce the dimension and obtain vectors such that $v_i.v_j \simeq M(v_i, v_j)$.

Consider the following 4 structured Amis sentences[5]:

Nika ina Hungti, mi-padang t-u   suwal n-ira   tatakulaq;
but   that King   AV-help   OBL-ART word GEN-that frog[6]
But as for the king, he supported the words of the frog;

"Isu Kungcu,   yu   ira k-u   pa-padang-an;
you Princess when   exist NOM-ART RED-help-LOC
"You Princess, when (you) had some help;

Sulinay mi-padang k-u   taw;
indeed   AV-help   NOM-ART people
indeed when people help;

aka-a   ka-pawan   t-u   ni-padang-an   n-u   taw."
PROH-IMP NFIN-forget OBL-ART PFV.NMZ-help-LOC GEN-ART people
then, you mustn't forget people's help."

---

[4]A word can have several prefixes and suffixes. In Figure 2, the most frequent pairs (prefixes;suffixes) are *(ma-;)*, i.e. the prefix *ma-* with no suffix, *(ka-;)*, i.e. the prefix *ka-* with no suffix, *(pa-se-;)*, i.e. the two prefixes *pa-* and *se-* with no suffix and *(ma;ay)*, i.e. the prefix *ma-* with the suffix *-ay*.

[5]The first line is the original text where words are structured as prefix-root-suffix. The second line is the morphological analysis with labels such as AV, OBL,....The third line is the translation.

[6]Abbreviations: AV Actor Voice; ART article; CV conveyanve voice; GEN genitive; IMP imperative; INST.V instrumental voice; LOC locative; LV locative voice; NFIN non-finite; NOM nominative; NMZ nominaliser; OBL oblique; PFV perfect; PROH prohibitive; RED reduplication; UV undergoer voice.

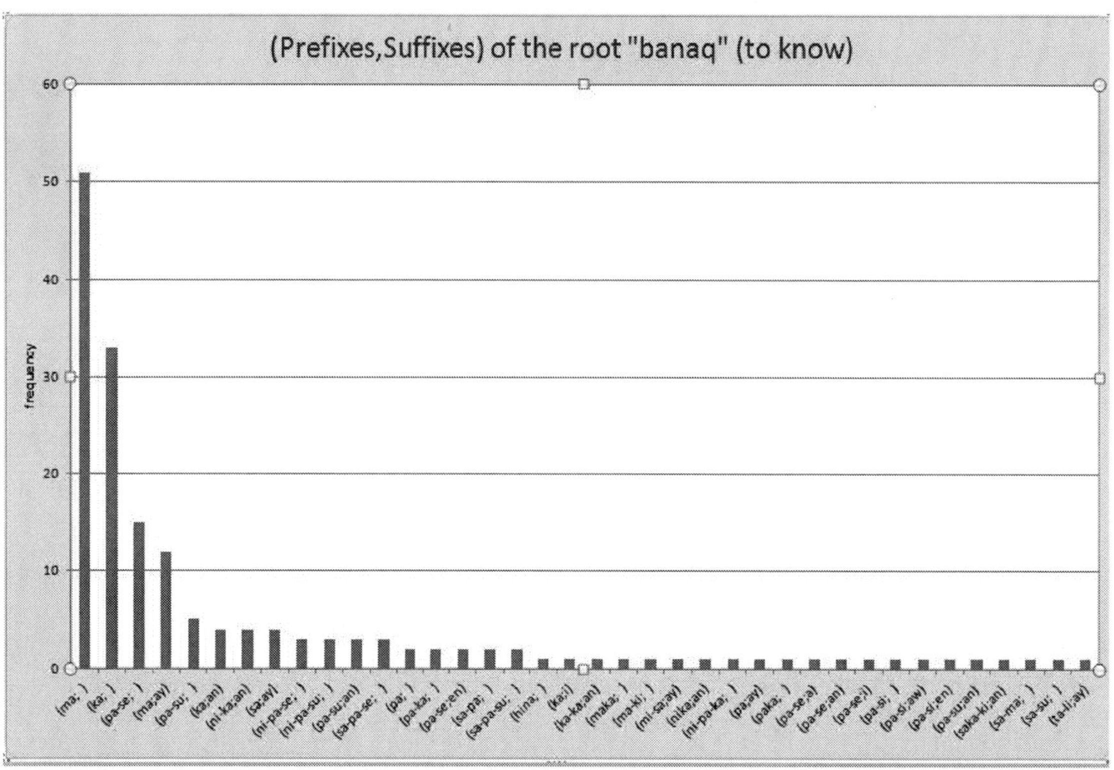

Figure 2: Most frequent (prefixes;suffixes) of the root *banaq* (' know').

In these sentences, there are seven prefixes: *k,ka,n,ni,mi,pa,t*. The matrix M_p for these prefixes is:

$$M_p = \begin{bmatrix} 4 & 0 & 0 & 2 & 0 & 2 & 0 \\ 0 & 2 & 2 & 2 & 0 & 0 & 2 \\ 0 & 2 & 4 & 2 & 2 & 0 & 4 \\ 2 & 2 & 2 & 4 & 0 & 0 & 2 \\ 0 & 0 & 2 & 0 & 2 & 0 & 2 \\ 2 & 0 & 0 & 0 & 0 & 2 & 0 \\ 0 & 2 & 4 & 2 & 2 & 0 & 4 \end{bmatrix}$$

The actual values in M_p are doubled to be consistent with the probability measure. The first line indicates 2 occurrences of *k-*, 1 occurrence of *k-, pa-* (second sentence) and 1 occurrence of *k-, mi-* (third sentence). The large eigenvalues of M_p are 6 and 3.2. Two other eigenvalues are close to 1 and the three others are close to 0. If we decompose the vectors[7] on the large eigenvectors, we obtain 7 vectors of dimension 2, one for each prefix.

$$B = \begin{bmatrix} 1.8860e + 00 & -4.7065e - 01 \\ -9.9611e - 17 & 6.5699e - 01 \\ -4.7150e - 01 & -2.8430e - 01 \\ 9.4301e - 01 & 9.6547e - 01 \\ -4.7150e - 01 & -9.4129e - 01 \\ 9.4301e - 01 & -7.7913e - 01 \\ -4.7150e - 01 & -2.8430e - 01 \end{bmatrix}$$

and $B * B^t$ is approximately M_p. In this example the absolute L_2 error is 11.5. The first vector for *k-* has coordinates $1.88, -0.47$. We can therefore represent graphically the 7 prefixes as in Figure 4. A similar approach can be followed for suffixes and for roots. Figure 4 can be used to predict, given a prefix v, the most likely next prefix v_{next}. It is the vector v' which maximizes the dot product $|v.v'|$. Given the vector for the prefix *k-*, the most likely next prefix is *pa-*.

---

[7]We used Octave, a tool for linear algebra to obtain the SVD decomposition and the projection.

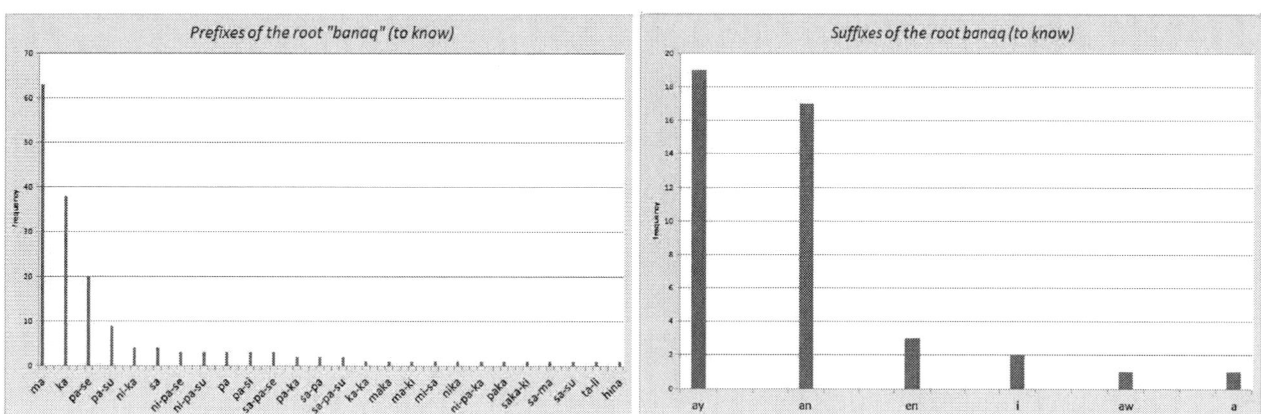

Figure 3: Most frequent prefixes and suffixes of the root *banaq*.

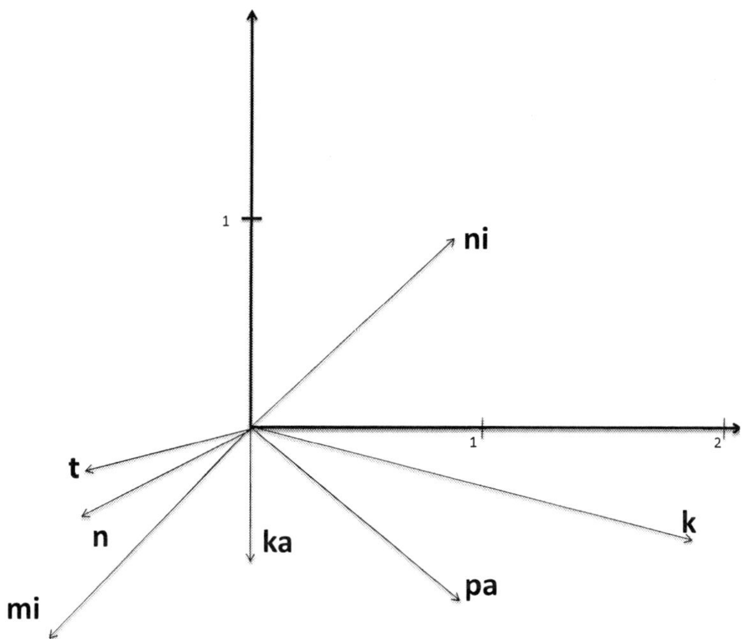

Figure 4: The vectors for the 7 most frequent prefixes *k-,ka-,n-,ni-,mi-,pa-,t-* in two dimensions.

3.3 Distributions and representative vectors

All the distributions are related, mostly by projections. Let δ be the distribution of the words, δ_P the distribution of the prefixes (resp. δ_R the distribution of the roots) and let π_p be the mapping which associates the prefix of a word. For example, $\pi_p(\textit{mi-padang})=\textit{mi-}$. Similarly $\pi_r(\textit{mi-padang})=\textit{padang}$. Then $\delta_P = \pi_p(\delta)$ and $\delta_R = \pi_r(\delta)$. Similarly for the other distributions. The correlation matrix M_p of the prefixes is also the projection of the correlation matrix M of the words, i.e. $M_p = \pi_p(M)$.

For each correlation matrix M_p, M_r, M_s, we apply the dimension reduction and obtain vectors $v_{p,i}$ of dimension n_p for the prefixes, $v_{r,i}$ of dimension n_r for the roots and $v_{s,i}$ of dimension n_s for the suffixes. We associate the union of the three vectors to a word $w=\textit{pre-root-suf}$:

$$\text{ustat}(w) = \begin{pmatrix} v_{p,pre} \\ v_{r,root} \\ v_{s,\text{suf}} \end{pmatrix}$$

For two words w_i, w_j, let $\widetilde{M}(w_i, w_j) = M_p(pre_i, pre_j) + M_r(root_i, root_j) + M_p(\text{suf}_i, \text{suf}_j)$ be the sum of the correlations of the prefixes, roots and suffixes. The fundamental fact of the approach is that for any two words w_i, w_j, $\text{ustat}(w_i).\text{ustat}(w_j) \simeq \widetilde{M}(w_i, w_j)$. Indeed, $\text{ustat}(w_i).\text{ustat}(w_j) = v_{p,pre_i}.v_{p,pre_j} + v_{r,root_i}.v_{r,root_j} + v_{s,suf_i}.v_{s,suf_j}$. The dot product $v_{p,pre_i}.v_{p,pre_j}$ approximates $M_p(pre_i, pre_j)$ and similarly for the roots and suffixes. Hence $\text{ustat}(w_i).\text{ustat}(w_j) \simeq \widetilde{M}(w_i, w_j)$.

Notice that $\widetilde{M}(w_i, w_j)$ can be very different from $M(w_i, w_j)$. It is possible that $M(w_i, w_j) = 0$, but that its prefixes, suffixes and roots have strong correlations, hence $\widetilde{M}(w_i, w_j)$ can be large. A rich theory of these structured vectors can be developed using cross-correlations, which we do not use at this point.

4   Grammars and statistics

We now study how to extend the vectors from words to sentences, as in Socher et al. (2010, 2013). We follow a different strategy as we fix a probabilistic *Content Vector* with specific dimensions which depend directly on the prefixes, roots and suffixes. We then show its use for a syntactic decomposition. A grammar G is classically represented by rules of the type[8]:

$$S \rightarrow VP.KP + VP.KP^*$$
$$VP \rightarrow Voice.V.KP^*$$
$$KP \rightarrow K.DP$$
$$DP \rightarrow D.N + D.N.ModP$$
$$ModP \rightarrow K.DP$$
$$K \rightarrow t + ...$$
$$V \rightarrow padang + ...$$
$$Voice \rightarrow mi + ...$$
$$N \rightarrow suwal + ...$$
$$D \rightarrow u + ...$$

Our goal is to compare the possible derivation trees of the sentence *mi-padang t-u suwal n-ira tatakulaq* and to use the *Content Vector* to infer the "most likely" tree in the grammar G.

4.1   Stochastic grammars

In a stochastic grammar Manning and Schütze (1999), derivations with the same non terminal symbol have a probability p such that the sum of the probabilities for each non terminal is 1. The probabilistic space associates with each sentence s and derivation tree t, the product of the probabilities of the rules used, noted $p(s, t)$. Given a sentence, a classical task is to predict the most likely derivation tree, and it can be achieved in $O(n^3)$ for a sentence of n words.

In our context, the probabilistic space is entirely different. The structured vectors allow us to predict the most likely word, prefix or suffix, given a context of previous words. They also determine the distribution of *Content Vector* defined in section 4.2 which predicts some key semantic components. Hence we look at the most likely derivation tree, given this distribution of semantic components.

4.2   Semantic representation

Let us define the *Content* vector of a sentence as a vector of dimension 6 whose components are:

- Valence: $\{0, 1, 2, 3\}$,

- Voice: {AV, UV, LV, INST.V},

- Tense: {Present, Past, Future},

- Mood: {Indicative, Imperative, Hortative, Subjunctive},

- Illocutionary Force: {Declarative, Negative, Exclamative},

- Information Structure: {Topicalisation, Cleft Focus},

---

[8]KP stands for Case Phrase, DP stands for Determiner Phrase, ModP stands for Modifier Phrase.

This is a just an example and more dimensions could be used. Let c be such vector of dimension 6 where values are distributions over each finite domain. For example, the third component c^3 over {Present, Past, Future} is $[0, 1, 0]$ to indicate a PAST or $[\frac{1}{3}, \frac{1}{3}, \frac{1}{3}]$ to indicate a uniform distribution. We read the sentence $w_1, w_2, ...w_n$, and a vector $v_i = \text{ustat}(w_i)$ is associated with each word w_i. Let us define:

$$c_i = F(c_{i-1}, v_i)$$

with c_0 an initial state and F a function, we construct by cases or by learning techniques. As an example, consider the following sentence:

tengil-i   isu   k-aku !
hear-IMP.UV GEN.2sg NOM-1sg
'listen to me !' (lit. let me be listened to by you)

In this case, the suffix *-i* expresses the imperative mood in Undergoer Voice. The suffix thus carries specific syntactic and semantic instructions, such as mood and UV voice, which itself encodes a type of alignment (a nominative patient pivot and a genitive agent). In this case c_i^2, the second component of F is defined as:

$$c_i^2(c_{i-1}, v_i) = \begin{cases} [0, 1, 0, 0] & \text{if } [v_i]_p = \text{"mi-"} \\ c_{i-1}^2 & \text{otherwise} \end{cases}$$

In general, each component of F is built as a decision tree, with rules and possible learnt components. At the end of a sentence, we have the Content vector c_n. We describe more advanced rules of *Amis* in section 4.4.

4.3   Rules and Correlations

The previous rule for the imperative mood is simple. It is also possible to learn this rule from positive and negative examples, i.e. sentences in imperative mood and sentences not in imperative mood, as suggested in Socher et al. (2013). In that case, we would get a correlation and a neural network could approximate the imperative mood given enough examples.

This is a general paradigm, often called *Causality versus Correlation*. It is however far more difficult to learn the structure of the Content vector, i.e. the decomposition in 6 independent components. Notice that 5 of the components are set by the prefixes and suffixes. The Valence is set by the roots. As the number of prefixes and suffixes is small, the description of the function F is much simplified.

4.4   A syntactic outline of Amis

The basic word order of Amis is predicate initial. Arguments are case-marked: nominative is marked by *k-*, the agent is marked as genitive by *n-*, oblique themes and oblique arguments are marked by *t-* Chen (1987). The voice affixes (AV) *mi-*, (UV) *ma-*, also identify verb classes, (i) verbs which only accept *mi-* voice, (ii) verbs which only accept *ma-*, (iii) verbs which accept both *mi-* and *ma-* with different semantics, and (iv) stative, property verb stems which accept none of these prefixes.

AV *mi-* verb stems denote activities or accomplishments. *Ma-* verbs denote non-actor or undergoer oriented events (depending on their semantics and valency); *ma-* verbs include states and psych states, properties, verbs of cognition (*ma-banaq* 'know'), bodily functions, position and motion[9] (*ma-nanuwang* 'move for object').

The root's ontology and semantic features pair up with the semantic and syntactic properties of voice affixes. The voice system is thus based on the co-selection of a nominative argument (the pivot), and a voice affix whose semantics matches the semantics of the nominative pivot. AV *mi-* and UV *ma-* voices are restricted to declarative sentences. In non-declarative sentences (such as negative, imperative, hortative), *mi-* occurs as *pi-* and *ma-* as *ka-*. Compare *ma-butiq cira* '(s)he is asleep/sleeping' and *ka-butiq!* 'go to sleep !'.

---

[9]Motion verbs are not activities despite their dynamic feature; their nominative pivot is not an Actor but a theme.

4.4.1 Transitivity and alignment

Alignment[10] varies with transitivity. *Mi-* verbs and extended intransitive *ma-* verbs (labelled Non-Actor Voice,NAV) have an oblique argument marked by *t-* as in (1a-2). The nominative pivot of *mi-* verbs is an Actor, while that of NAV *ma-* verbs is a Non-Actor (i.e. a theme or experiencer, the seat of some property or state). On the other hand, transitive UV *ma-* verbs have a nominative (generally fully affected) patient pivot and a genitive agent as in (1b).

    1a. *Mi-melaw k-u   wawa t-u   tilibi.*
      AV-look   NOM-ART child OBL-ART TV
      ' The child is watching TV. '

    1b. *Ma-melaw n-uhni   k-u   teker.*
      UV-look   GEN-3pl NOM-ART trap
      'They saw the trap.'(lit. the trap was seen by him)

    2. *Ma-hemek   k-aku   t-u   babainay. (*mi-)*
      NAV-admire NOM-1sg OBL-ART boy
      'I admire the guy.'

Ma- verbs are thus generally oriented towards a non-actor, or an undergoer nominative pivot; the case assignment of the non-pivot argument varies with transitivity: with extended intransitive NAV *ma-* constructions (2), the theme is oblique; with transitive UV *ma-* constructions, the agent is genitive (1b). All other voices, UV *-en*, INST *sa-*, LOC *-an*, CV *si-*, have a nominative pivot which is the corresponding semantic argument (i.e. patient, instrument, location, transported theme), and a genitive Agent (if it is expressed).

4.5 Best derivation tree

Given c_n, we can then decide that the (a) derivation tree of Figure 5 is better suited than the (b) for the sentence *mi-padang t-u suwal n-ira tatakulaq* ('he supports the words of the frog'). We follow the explanation of the *mi-* verbs given in section 4.4.

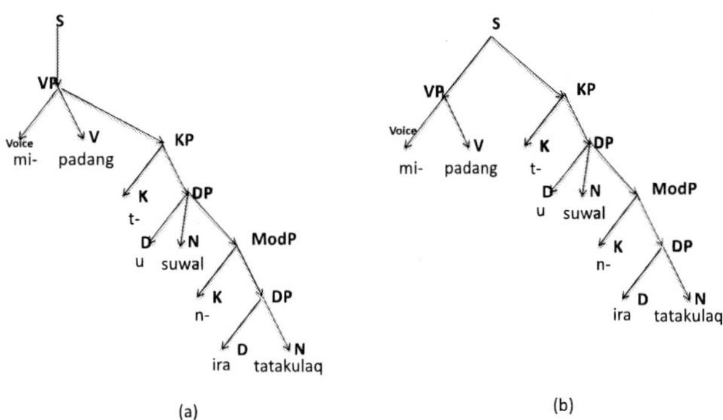

Figure 5: Tree derivations of the sentence *mi-padang t-u suwal n-ira tatakulaq* for the grammar G.

The conceptual structure of a verb stem selects the voice, the number and type of arguments. Case-assignment takes place in the domain of the VP and correlates with Voice which assigns theta-roles to its arguments (for ex. an AV mi-verb

---

[10]Alignment refers to the morphosyntactic encoding of the grammatical relationship between the two arguments of transitive verbs, and the single argument of intransitive verbs. In accusative languages, the subjects are marked in the same way independently of transitivity, and differently from the object. In ergative languages, the single argument of intransitive verbs and the patient of transitive verbs are similarly marked as nominative/absolutive, but differently from the agent of transitive verbs.

assigns nominative to the Actor and oblique to the theme; an UV ma-verb assigns nominative to the Patient and genitive to the agent). Consequently the derivation tree (a) is a better representation.

5 Conclusion

We introduced a statistical model for the morphology of natural languages and applied it to *Amis*. The *Morphix* tool builds the classical distributions of prefixes, roots and suffixes, given a possible root, prefix or suffix. From the second moments of the distributions, we build vectors for prefixes, roots and suffixes which capture their correlations. There are about 30 most common suffixes, and 15 of them carry 90% of the mass. Among the 10 most common suffixes, 4 of them carry 90% of the mass. Hence, the dimensions of the corresponding vectors are small.

We defined a probabilistic *Content vector* as a simplified model for the semantic and syntactic analysis of a sentence. The online analysis of the prefixes and suffixes, realised by the function F, determines most of the components of the *Content* vector c. Given a grammar G and a sentence $w_1, w_2, ...w_n$, we then looked at the most likely tree decomposition for c.

Other languages have different types of morphology or no morphology, but we argue that the most likely tree decomposition is dependent on semantic features in a probabilistic way.

References

Baayen, R. (2008). *Analyzing Linguistic Data: A Practical Introduction to Statistics using R*. Cambridge University Press.

Blust, R. (1999). Subgrouping, circularity and extinction: Some issues in austronesian comparative linguistics. In E. Zeitoun and P. Li (Eds.), *Selected Papers from the Eighth International Conference on Austronesian Linguistics*, pp. 31–94. Taipei: Institute of Linguistics, Academia Sinica.

Bril, I. (2017). Roots and stems: Lexical and functional flexibility in amis and nêlêmwa. In E. van Lier (Ed.), *Studies in Language. Special issue on lexical flexibility in Oceanic languages (In Press)*, pp. 358–407.

Chen, T. (1987). Verbal constructions and verbal classifications in nataoran-amis. In *Series C. Canberra: Pacific linguistics*.

Manning, C. D. and H. Schütze (1999). *Foundations of Statistical Natural Language Processing*. Cambridge, MA, USA: MIT Press.

Mikolov, T., K. Chen, G. Corrado, and J. Dean (2013). Efficient estimation of word representations in vector space. *CoRR abs/1301.3781*.

Ross, M. (2009). Proto austronesian verbal morphology: a reappraisal. In A. Adelaar and A. Pawley (Eds.), *Austronesian historical linguistics and culture history. A festschrift for Robert Blust*, pp. 285–31. Canberra: Pacific Linguistics.

Sagart, L. (2004). The higher phylogeny of austronesian and the position of tai-kadai. *Oceanic Linguistics 43*, 411–444.

Socher, R., J. Bauer, C. D. Manning, and A. Y. Ng (2013). Parsing with compositional vector grammars. In *In Proceedings of the ACL conference*.

Socher, R., C. D. Manning, and A. Y. Ng (2010). Learning continuous phrase representations and syntactic parsing with recursive neural networks. In *In Proceedings of the NIPS-2010 Deep Learning and Unsupervised Feature Learning Workshop*.

Developing LexO: a Collaborative Editor of Multilingual Lexica and Termino-Ontological Resources in the Humanities

Andrea Bellandi,
Emiliano Giovannetti, Silvia Piccini
Istituto di Linguistica Computazionale - CNR
`{name.surname}@ilc.cnr.it`

Anja Weingart
Georg-August-Universität Göttingen
`aweinga@gwdg.de`

Abstract

In this paper we present a first version of LexO, a collaborative editor of multilingual lexica and termino-ontological resources. It is based on the *lemon* model, and aims at supporting lexicographers and terminologists in their work. Although the development of LexO is still ongoing, the editor is already being used within two research projects in the field of Computational Linguistics applied to Humanities: DiTMAO and Totus Mundus. This allowed to test the functionalities of LexO and to prove its high degree of flexibility according to the different extensions of the *lemon* model needed to fulfill the needs of the involved scholars.

1   Introduction

This paper describes the ongoing development of LexO, a web collaborative editor of lexical and termino-ontological resources based on the *lemon* model[1]. As it will be described later, LexO provides some peculiar features (such as references to texts and extensibility) that make it particularly suited to be used in the Humanities.

Nowadays, well-founded lexico-semantic models designed during the last two decades enable to build lexical resources providing a rich description of word meaning with a view to retrieving and processing lexical data in texts. The main models are: WordNet (Fellbaum, 1998), Framenet (Fillmore et al., 2003), Pattern Dictionary (Hanks and Pustejovsky, 2005), SIMPLE (Lenci et al., 2000) and Brandeis Semantic Ontology (Pustejovsky, 2006). Strongly inspired by the lexical model SIMPLE, the metamodel Lexical Markup Framework (LMF) (Gil Francopoulo and Soria, 2006) was created to provide a common model to represent and encode lexical resources, and to ensure interoperability among them.

As far as the terminological perspective is concerned, the ISO standard TMF - Terminological Markup Framework - was created in 2003 (Romary, 2001). This abstract model for the representation of multilingual terminological data was introduced to cover two concurrent standards: MARTIF (Machine-readable terminology interchange format, also known as ISO (FDIS) 12200) and GENETER, which belong to SALT family of data models and formats. Over the last years, however, terminologists have started to adopt models developed within the field of lexicology, in order to describe the relationships between terms in a richer way. In fact, the traditional methodologies for describing terms, focused on the analysis of conceptual aspects (onomasiological perspective), have led terminologists to take into account only taxonomic and meronymic relationships. Differently, lexicographic models, based on a semasiological, word-oriented approach, take into account a richer set of relevant relationships. This is why, for example, (Dancette and L'Homme, 2004) propose to convert specialized dictionaries using a formal lexico-semantic framework called Explanatory and Combinatorial Lexicology (ECL), developed by (Mel'čuk et al., 1995) in the framework of the Meaning-Text approach.

---

[1]In this paper we assume that the reader is already familiar with *lemon*. For an exhaustive description of the model, the reader is reffered to: http://*lemon*-model.net/ (last access: 17/07/2017)

The editor we here present, called LexO, is being developed with the objective of supporting both lexicographers and terminologists in their work of building, respectively, lexica and termino-ontological resources. This is the primary reason we chose *lemon* as LexO's underlying lexical model: *lemon* is the most recent model proposed in the field of Computational Lexicography which displays some characteristics that were deemed suitable for both lexicographers and terminologists. Firstly, *lemon* is based on LMF, the ISO standard used for lexica supporting Natural Language Processing (NLP) tasks and Machine Readable Dictionaries (MRD) and which has already been used to model a number of other important lexical resources such as the Princeton Wordnet, Framenet and Verbnet. Secondly, *lemon* was proposed to provide a standard for representing multilingual lexical resources using Semantic web technologies such as RDF and OWL. Finally, in *lemon* the conceptual and linguistic dimensions are separated but interconnected. The link between lexical entries and ontological concepts is reified through the class Lexical sense.

In terminology distinguishing between lexical and conceptual dimension is proven to be fundamental, at least from a methodological point of view, especially when addressing very different languages. The theoretical necessity of distinguishing between these two levels has led to the development of new paradigms (Roche, Roche), and strategies (Reymonet et al., 2007). While, typically, a lexicon is the inventory of the words (or lexemes) of a certain language, a termino-ontological resource is composed of terms of a specific domain which are related to concepts structured in a formal ontology describing that domain.

The paper is structured as follows. In Section 2 an overview is given of existing tools designed to handle lexica and termino-ontological resources. Section 3 describes the key characteristics of LexO and its architecture. In Section 4 two projects in which the tool is being used are described. Finally, Section 5 draws some conclusion and outlines what we are currently working on to improve the editor.

2   Existing editors

Concerning lexicon and terminology editors, several tools have already been proposed.

Lexus[2] (Ringersma and Kemps-Snijders, 2007) is a collaborative Web-based lexicon tool developed at the Max Planck Institute for Psycholinguistics. It allows users to create lexica in LMF using the concept naming conventions of ISO data categories. It provides functionalities to include audio, video and still images to the lexicon. With Lexus, users can share lexica and define filters to visualize the entries. Lexus is freely available for use to registered users. Coldic (Núria Bel and Villegas, 2008) is a Web-based lexicographic platform. Similarly to Lexus, it manages LMF lexica. Coldic consists of a database, a graphical interface for the lexicographer and a web services interface. Among its features we cite the automatic generation of a graphical view of the lexical model that is used as a support in the query builder tool. Though released as open source, Coldic is no longer maintained. In addition, Coldic is a single-user tool, i.e. it cannot be used to create lexica in a collaborative way. On the contrary, Wordnet Editor (Szymanski, 2009) was conceived to be cooperative and graphical-oriented. The main goal of the project, carried out at the Gdansk University of Technology, was to create a system providing an easy-to-use interface for WordNet content navigation and editing in an interactive way. A demo version[3] should be available online, but at present the editing features are not accessible and the whole project seems discontinued. Another web editor is PoolParty (Schandl and Blumauer, 2010), a tool for the management of thesauri as Linked Data. PoolParty supports SKOS[4] and has an optional add-on for SKOS-XL. PoolParty allows users to model a vocabulary in RDFS or OWL, either locally or by importing it from external sources. *lemon* source is a Wiki-like site for manipulating and publishing *lemon* data aimed at the collaborative development of lexical resources. It makes it possible to upload a lexicon and share it with others. *lemon* source is an open source project, based on the *lemon* API, and it is freely available online for use. Regarding the *lemon* model, we also cite (Fiorelli et al., 2017), an editor

[2]http://tla.mpi.nl/tools/tla-tools/lexus (last access: 17/07/2017)

[3]http://wordventure.eti.pg.gda.pl/wne/wne.html (last access: 17/07/2017)

[4]https://www.w3.org/2004/02/skos/ (last access: 17/07/2017)

with custom forms to support in the construction of *lemon*. It is an extension of VocBench, a web-based collaborative thesaurus editing and workflow system, natively supporting Semantic Web standards such as RDF, OWL and SKOS(-XL).

Concerning terminologies, there are several commercial Computer-Assisted Translation softwares which integrate components dedicated to terminology management, such as, for example, Trados[5] and Multitrans[6]. It is worth mentioning also the LexGrid Editor (Johnson et al., 2005), a tool developed by the Division of Biomedical Informatics Research of the Mayo Clinic providing the capability to author, view, validate, maintain and extend terminologies defined on the basis of the LexGrid terminology model. An editor designed for constructing corpus-based lexica is CoBaLT (Kenter et al., 2012). This web-based tool has been used to compile a large lexicon of historical Slovene and it manages importing and exporting in TEI P5.

Existing tools allowing users to edit resources on both lexical and ontological levels are very few. The Neon Toolkit[7] has been exploited by LabelTranslator, a tool developed by (Espinoza et al., 2008) in the form of a plug-in to support the LIR (Linguistic Information Repository) model. The tool provides a set of linguistic elements for localizing ontological elements. TextViz (Reymonet et al., 2007) is an editor taking explicitly into consideration references to a textual corpus. It has been developed as another plug-in, this time for the Protégé-OWL framework. TextViz is a visual annotation environment for the construction of Ontological and Terminological Resources (OTR) in the OWL-DL model. TemaTres[8] is an open source web application for the management of controlled vocabularies. It adopts a series of Semantic Web technologies for the representation of controlled vocabularies, thesauri, taxonomies and formal representations of knowledge. Lastly, we cite Tedi[9] (ontoTerminology EDItor), a tool in development at the University Savoie Mont Blanc for the construction of so called "ontoterminologies", defined as terminologies whose conceptual system is a formal ontology.

3 Distinctive characteristics of LexO

As emerges from the previous overview, editors of lexical, terminological or termino-ontological resources are not so widespread and do not always display at the same time all the requirements scholars working in the humanities consider crucial. In many cases, scholars are forced to adopt ontology editors, such as Pinakes (Bozzi and Scotti, 2015) and *Protégé*, to formalize their lexical or terminological resources. As a result, LexO is conceived to have all characteristics we list below. These features were defined on the basis of the experience gained in the creation of lexica and terminological resources in the framework of several projects in the field of Digital Humanities, see (Piccini and Ruimy, 2015), and (Piccini et al., 2016). We do not claim that this list is exhaustive; more features can be added in the future, thanks to the flexible architecture of LexO.

- Ease of use: the editor is meant to be used mainly by humanists and, thus, hide all the technical complexities related to markup languages, language formalities and other technology issues. To make an example, the creation of a new (*lemon*) lexical entry requires a single press of a button: the system, "under the hood", creates a new instance of the LexicalEntry class of the specified lexicon, a new form, a new lexical sense, and all the necessary relationships holding among them.

- Collaborativeness: LexO, being a web application, makes collaborative editing possible. The collaborative construction process of lexical resources offers very promising research opportunities in the context of electronic lexicography. As a matter of fact, a team of users, each one with his/her own role (lexicographers, domain experts, scholars, etc.), can work on the same resource collaboratively. As a result, resources quickly increase in size and are constantly updated. In

---

[5]http://www.sdltrados.com/ (last access: 17/07/2017)

[6]https://www.multitranstms.com (last access: 17/07/2017)

[7]http://neon-toolkit.org/wiki/Main_Page (last access: 17/07/2017)

[8]http://www.vocabularyserver.com/ (last access: 17/07/2017)

[9]http://christophe-roche.fr/tedi (last access: 17/07/2017)

addition, the automatic consistency checking supported by OWL reasoners can play a crucial role when lexical resources are constructed collaboratively in order to avoid possible "conflicting" assertions.

- Sharing and linking: the editor adheres to international standards for representing lexica and ontologies in the Semantic Web (such as *lemon* and OWL), so that lexical resources can be shared easily or specific entities can be linked to existing datasets.

- Reference to texts: the linking of lexical entries to specific portions of texts (i.e. attestations) is a typical linguistic and philological requirement: lexicographers and terminologists may create their lexical (or terminological) resources from texts; although currently in progress, LexO intends to provide features to link each entity of the resource (being it a form, a term, a concept, etc.) to a text or to a very specific portion of a text, via canonical references mechanisms such as CTS (Tiepmar et al., 2014). Appropriate extensions of the *lemon* model are being developed to represent attestations.

- Extensibility: conceived to handle historical and ancient lexica and terminologies as well, the editor is flexible and extensible enough to formalize peculiar features of such linguistic resources. Among the first major extensions we are currently working on, we cite diachrony and attestation, the first to be implemented by starting from the already available *lemon*-DIA (Khan et al., 2014) and the second one from the work by (Bellandi et al., 2017). It is worth underlying that the process of extension in LexO is facilitated by the fact that also *lemon*, the lexical model of reference, is designed to be modular and to integrate new components easily.

These two latter features make LexO particularly suited to be applied in Humanities, although it may be used by lexicographers and terminologists in general.

With regard to the *lemon* lexical model, we adopted an in-memory persistency solution by exploiting the OWL-API 5.0, a Java API and reference implementation for creating, manipulating and serialising OWL ontologies.

Here we present a first version of LexO. Not all the characteristics listed at the beginning of this Section have already been developed. From the technical point of view, currently data consistency is implemented at user interface level and a reasoner has not yet been set up. In addition, it must be underlined that the in-memory persistence we adopted is not a scalable strategy in case the resource size increases considerably. However, we successfully tested this version of LexO within two research projects aiming at encoding multilingual lexica and termino-ontological resources. The usage of the tool is documented in the next Section, but here we provide an overview of the main interface. It is composed of 4 columns (see the center of Figure 1 and 2). The leftmost column allows scholars to browse lemmas, forms and senses, according to the *lemon* model. By clicking one of them, the system shows the lexical entry of reference in the second column alongside the lemma and its forms, and, in the third one, the relative lexical senses. A user can annotate linguistic and lexicographic properties concerning the lemmatization of terms, such as script types, transliterations and types of variants (see 4.1), and lexico-semantic relations between senses, such as synonymy and translation (see Section 4.1, and Section 4.2) or link a sense to the concept of an ontology of reference (see Section 4.2). The last column, which can be shown or hidden, is used to show the details of the lexical entry which is linked to another one by means of a specific relation.

4   Use Cases

In the next subsections, we show our tool in action within the framework of two projects: DiTMAO and Totus Mundus.

4.1 The DiTMAO Project

LexO is being developed in the context of the project "Dictionnaire de Termes Médico-botaniques de l'Ancien Occitan" (DiTMAO[10]), which aims at constructing an ontology-based information system for Old Occitan medico-botanical terminology. Old Occitan is the medieval stage of Occitan, the autochthonous Romance language spoken in Southern France, today regional minority language with several dialects. During the Middle Ages, the region and its language played a significant role in medical science due to the medical schools of Toulouse and Montpellier and the strong presence of Jewish physicians and scholars. For this reason, Old Occitan medico-botanical terminology is documented both in Latin, Hebrew and Arabic characters (ben Isaak et al., 2011).

The textual basis of DiTMAO lexicon, as described in (Corradini and Mensching, 2010) and (Bos, Corradini, and Mensching, Bos et al.), consists of medico-botanical texts in Latin and in Hebrew script. Among the sources in Hebrew script, the most prominent text type are so-called synonym lists. These lists can be described as ancient multilingual dictionaries, which contain a large amount of Old Occitan medical and botanical terms in Hebrew characters with equivalents or explanations in other languages (also spelled in Hebrew characters), mostly in (Judaeo-)Arabic, but also in Hebrew, Latin, and sometimes in Aramaic (Mensching, 2004), (Mensching, 2009) and (ben Isaak et al., 2011). A special difficulty of medieval texts in vernacular languages is that most terms are documented in a large number of variants (reflecting different spellings, dialects, or historical stages of the languages at issue). The particularities of the DiTMAO corpus (medieval, multilingual and multi-alphabetical) made the lemmatization a complex and intriguing issue (Corradini and Mensching, 2007), (Corradini and Mensching, 2010), and (Corradini, 2014). At date of submission, DiTMAO contains 1758 Old Occitan lemma forms and 1854 variants in Latin script, and 1378 variants in Hebrew script; 305 corresponding terms in Hebrew, 625 terms in Arabic, 77 terms in Latin, 29 terms in Aramaic and 21 mixed terms. Whenever, possible translations into modern French and English are provided.

The DiTMAO project aims at making this terminology accessible to several scientific communities, such as those of Romance and Semitic studies, as well as that of the history of medicine. In order to be useful for an interdisciplinary research community, the terminology should not only be accessible via the lemmata, but also via the meaning or conceptual side of the terms. In traditional Old Occitan lexicography, and in traditional lexicography in general, these two ways of accessing the terminology correspond to two main types of dictionaries: (i) alphabetically ordered dictionaries, such as (Stempel et al., 1997), and onomasiological dictionaries, such as (Baldinger et al., 2005). In onomasiological dictionaries, the terms are grouped according to their meaning and conceptual relations. The lemon model naturally combines these two types of dictionaries. The terminology can be classified according to formal, linguistic criteria and according to the semantics of the terms in an ontology. As the lemon model is designed for modern language lexica, several domain specific extensions had to be defined in order to be suitable for a historical dictionary. The extensions concern the linguistic and conceptual domain as well as the addition of an attestation domain (Weingart and Giovannetti, 2016).

In the following, an example is presented, showing how LexO satisfies the requirements and the workflow of historical (Old Occitan) lexicography, with focus on the lemmatization. The screenshot shows the lemma entry of mandragora, meaning "mandrake", in the red box and one (of many) variants in Hebrew script in the blue box. Due to space limitations, we will focus only on the formal properties of a lemma and its graphical, morpho-phonological or alphabetical variants. A lemma and a variant form have the following common properties, which are domain specific extensions (marked by*) or categories taken from the Lexinfo ontology[11], an extension of lemon that provides data categories for linguistic annotations. The common properties are: "Alphabet" [I*] with the option for Latin, Hebrew or Arabic, the "Transliteration" [II*], which is active in the variant box, showing the transliteration

---

[10]DiTMAO is a joint project of the PIs Gerrit Bos (Universität zu Köln), Emiliano Giovannetti (Istituto di Linguistica Computazionale "Antonio Zampolli" of the CNR), Maria Sofia Corradini (Università di Pisa) and Guido Mensching (Georg-August-Universität Göttingen). The project is funded by the Deutsche Forschungsgemeinschaft (DFG). Project web page: https://www.uni-goettingen.de/en/487498.html

[11]http://www.lexinfo.net/ontology/2.0/lexinfo.owl (last access: 17/07/2017)

MDRˀGWLH of the hebrew variant. Further, both can be annotated for "Part of speech", "Number" and "Gender" [III]. The "Documented In" field [IV*] shows the corpus-internal attestation. The lemma form has, in addition, the property of "Other documentation" [V*] for a corpus-external attestation. This is particularly important for two reasons: first, there is additional evidence for the meaning of a term in corpus-external sources and secondly, many terms are only documented in Hebrew script and in this case a corpus-external lemma or a reconstructed form will be used. The type of lemma can be indicated at the "Info" [VI*] drop down menu. The variant types [VII*] are also a domain specific extension. The variant MDRˀGWLH is read as "*madragolha" and differs from the lemma with respect to grapho-phonetic properties, in addition to difference in alphabet. In the yellow box, the semantic relations (translations, corresponding terms), and the conceptual link to the ontology can be managed. Furthermore, for plant names the external sources often mention the binominal scientific name, here Mandragora officinarum L., which is conceived similar to a translation. The leftmost column shows the navigation, which eases the reviewing process by the listing, sorting and counting options.

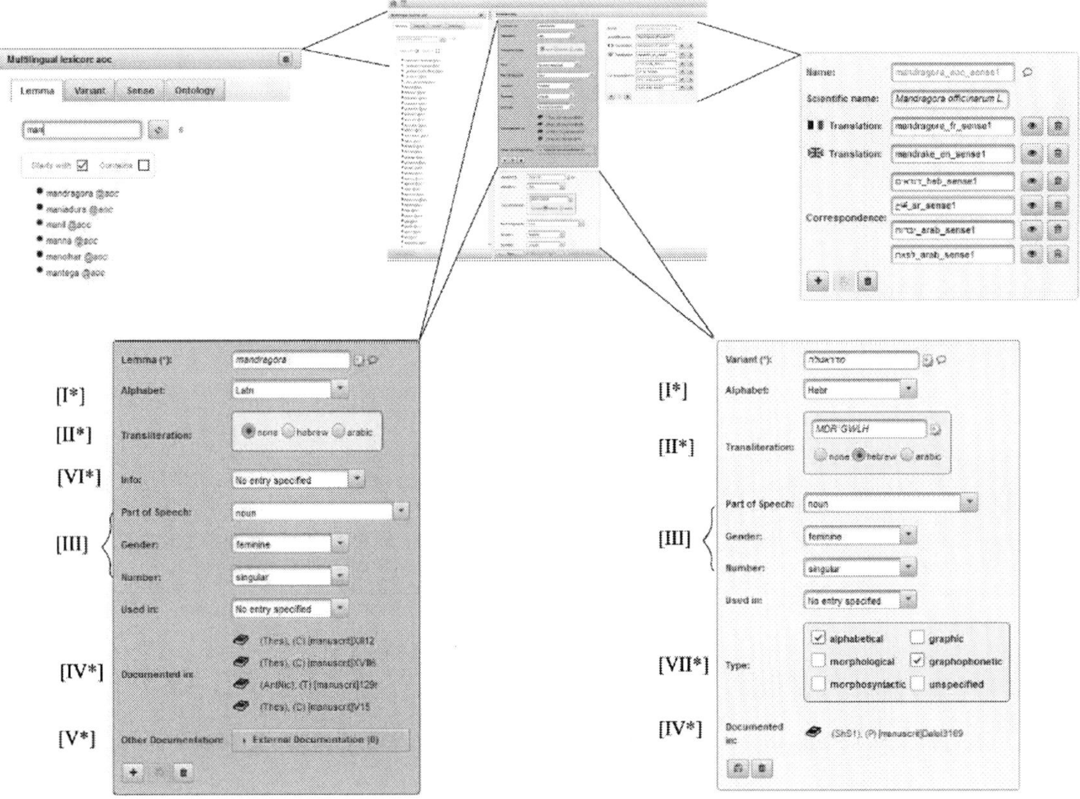

Figure 1: The components of LexO interface. Mandragora entry example.

4.2 The Totus Mundus Project

LexO has been adopted also in the framework of the Italian Project "Todo el mundo es nuestra casa. The World is Our Home. A virtual Journey Around the World Atlas by Matteo Ricci, SJ (1602)" (abbreviated in "Totus Mundus"), coordinated by Elisabetta Corsi, Chair Professor of Sinology at the University La Sapienza (Rome) and conducted in collaboration with the Historical Archives of the Pontifical Gregorian University (APUG) in Rome and the Institute of Informatics and Telematics (IIT) of the CNR in Pisa. The main objective of this project is to take users on a virtual journey through Matteo Ricci's world map and through its translation into Italian made by the Jesuit sinologist Pasquale D'Elia in 1938 and preserved at APUG. D'Elia's work is based on the third edition of the map created by Ricci in 1602 in Beijing in collaboration with the Chinese mathematician and astronomer Li Zizhao (1565-1630) and titled *Kunyu Wanguo Quantu* ("A Map of the Myriad Countries of the World"). This third version, made to stand on six folding screens and to engulf its observer, is the earliest to survive and the first to have given the Chinese a larger cosmological and geographical vision of the earth.

As a matter of fact, the map includes images and annotations describing different regions of the world as well as explanations regarding conceptions of systems of the terrestrial and celestial world. In order to make it possible for scholars to access the Chinese and Italian texts on a semantic basis, a termino-ontological bilingual resource has been developed, where the conceptual and the linguistic layers are separated but intimately linked, in accordance with the paradigms and the methodologies developed over the last few years (see Section 1).

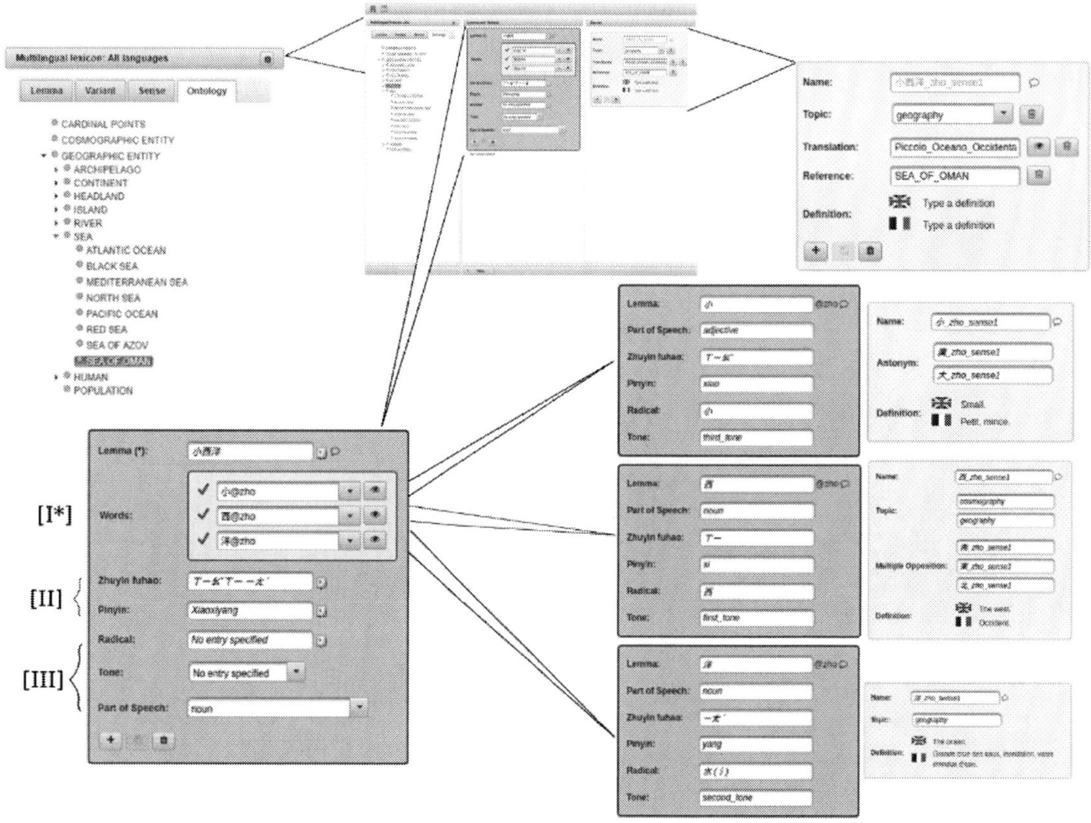

Figure 2: The components of LexO interface. The Little Western Ocean entry example.

The lexical component has been modeled in *lemon* and constructed with LexO, while the conceptual component has been structured into a formal ontology using *Protégé*. The taxonomy has been imported into LexO as well, in order to link each lexical sense to a concept of the ontology (see example in Figure 2). Compared to DitMAO lexicon, the size of Totus Mundus lexicon is smaller, as the project is still in its early stages. It currently contains 81 Chinese lexical entries (52 words and 29 multiwords) and 78 Italian lexical entries (61 words and 17 multiwords), which were extracted manually by the experts. Chinese terms are provided with French and English definitions, drawn respectively from the *Dictionnaire classique de la langue chinoise* by F. S. Couvreur S.J. and *the Chinese-English Dictionary* by the Australian Congregational Missionary R.H. Mathews.

Due to the flexible and modular architecture of the *lemon* model, classes and relationships have been easily customized in order to better meet the specific needs posed by the Chinese language. It must be emphasized that adapting *lemon* to seventeenth-century Chinese language constitutes a challenge and an interesting subject for reflection. Extensions were introduced, such as: i) the OWL class "ProsodicProperty", which subsumes the class "Tone", whose four different tones constitute the instances; ii) the Data property "radical", which refers to the graphical (and often semantic) component of Chinese characters, used to organise and list words in a Chinese dictionary; iii) two sub-properties of the Data Property "representation", i.e. "pinyinTransliteration" and "zhuyinFuhaoTransliteration". An example of Chinese lexical entry is illustrated in Figure 2, i.e. the multiword *Xiao xi yang* (litt. "The Little Western Ocean"). In the red box the three lexemes which compose the multiword are shown (I); *xiao* "little", *xi* "west", *yang* "ocean". By clicking on the eye near each lexical entry, on the rightmost column users can visualize the morphological properties as well as all the information concerning the lexical sense of the lexical entries the multiword is composed of. Specifically, in the red box Pinyin and Zhuyin Fuhao Transliterations are provided (II) and the morphological features are detailed such as Part of Speech, Tone, and Radical (III). The word sense is described in the yellow box: French and English definitions are given and lexical relations are also represented (for example synonymy, antonymy etc.) as well as the translation into Italian made by Pasquale D'Elia. The lexical sense is linked through the relation "reference" to an ontology concept. Geographic terminology has changed over time and ancient denominations result sometimes quite obscure especially for users who are not experts in this domain of knowledge. As a result, the ontology linking plays a crucial role, as it makes it possible to understand which geographic entity (sea, island, mountain, continent etc.) was designated by a certain term.

As we can see in Figure 2, *Xiao xi yang* was the ancient denomination of the sea of Oman. The concept is formally described in an ontology which has been built in *Protégé*.

LexO offers also the opportunity to link each lexical sense to external resources such as dBpedia, Wikipedia etc., in accordance with the Semantic Web philosophy.

5   Conclusion

In this paper we presented a first version of LexO, a collaborative editor of multilingual lexica and termino-ontological resources, based on the lemon model. The editor has been created to support lexicographers and terminologists in their work. Despite the fact that the development of LexO is still ongoing, the editor is already being used within two research projects: DiTMAO and Totus Mundus. Adopting LexO in these projects has allowed us to prove its high flexibility, since extensions of the lemon model were introduced easily, to fulfill the needs of the involved scholars.

We are currently focusing our research in the inclusion of other characteristics, such as the diachronic and diatopic variation of both lexical and conceptual aspects as well as the reference to texts. Regarding the ontological level, we plan to enhance LexO with multiple ontology editing. As another major update we want to allow users to create their own extensions of the lemon schema directly inside LexO and to have the interface automatically adapting to the customized model, similarly to what has been done by the team working on VocBench. As soon as it will be stable and documented enough, we plan to release LexO for the community.

Acknowledgment

This research has been partially funded by the DFG in the context of the cooperation agreement between prof. Guido Mensching, director of the DiTMAO project at the Seminar für Romanische Philologie of the Georg-August-Universität Göttingen and the Istituto di Linguistica Computazionale "A. Zampolli" of the Italian National Research Council (August 29th, 2016).

References

Baldinger, K., N. Winkler, and T. Shabafrouz (2005). *Dictionnaire onomasiologique de l'ancien occitan: DAO*. Niemeyer.

Bellandi, A., F. Boschetti, F. Khan, A. M. Del Grosso, and M. Monachini (2017). Provando e riprovando modelli di dizionario storico digitale: collegare voci, citazioni, interpretazioni. In *AIUCD 2017 Conference - Book of Abstracts*, pp. 119–125.

ben Isaak, S. T., G. Bos, and M. Hussein (2011). *Medical Synonym Lists from Medieval Provence: Shem Tov Ben Isaac of Tortosa: Sefer Ha-Shimmush. Book 29: Part1: Edition and Commentary of List 1 (Hebrew-Arabic-Romance/Latin)*, Volume 1. Brill.

Bos, G., M. Corradini, and G. Mensching. Le ditmao (dictionnaire des termes médico-botaniques de l'ancien occitan): caractères et organisation des données lexicales. *In Proceedings of the XIen Congrès de l'Asociacion Internacionala d'Estudis Occitans (AIEO)*.

Bozzi, A. and A. Scotti (2015). Pinakes e pinakes text : due strumenti per l'archiviazione, lo studio e l'interrogazione di documenti digitali di cultura. In *Reti in rete : per l'inventario e l'edizione dell'Archivio Vallisneri. S. Olschki, Firenze*, pp. 31–52.

Corradini, M. S. (2014). Lessico e tassonomia nell'organizzazione del dictionnaire de termes médico-botaniques de l'ancien occitan (ditmao). *In Revue de linguistique romane* (309-310), 87–132.

Corradini, M. S. and G. Mensching (2007). Les méthodologies et les outils pour la rédaction d'un lexique de la terminologie médico-botanique de l'occitan du moyen âge. *In Actes du XXVe Congrès International de Linguistique et de Philologie Romanes 6*, 87–96.

Corradini, M. S. and G. Mensching (2010). Nuovi aspetti relativi al dictionnaire de termes médico-botaniques de l'ancien occitan (ditmao): creazione di una base di dati integrata con organizzazione onomasiologica. In *Actas del XXVI Congreso Internacional de Lingüística y de Filología Románicas*, Volume 8, pp. 113–124.

Dancette, J. and M.-C. L'Homme (2004). Building specialized dictionaries using lexical functions. *Linguistica Antverpiensia, New Series–Themes in Translation Studies* (3), 113–131.

Espinoza, M., A. Gómez-Pérez, and E. Mena (2008). *LabelTranslator - A Tool to Automatically Localize an Ontology*, pp. 792–796.

Fellbaum, C. (1998). *WordNet: An Electronic Lexical Database*. Language, Speech, and Communication. Cambridge, MA: MIT Press.

Fillmore, C. J., C. R. Johnson, and M. R. Petruck (2003). Background to FrameNet. *International Journal of Lexicography 16.3*, 235–250.

Fiorelli, M., T. Lorenzetti, M. T. Pazienza, and A. Stellato (2017). *Assessing VocBench Custom Forms in Supporting Editing of Lemon Datasets*, pp. 237–252.

Gil Francopoulo, Monte George, N. C. M. M. N. B. m. P. and C. Soria (2006). Lexical markup framework (lmf). In *Proceedings of LREC2006, Genoa, Italy*.

Hanks, P. and J. Pustejovsky (2005). A pattern dictionary for natural language processing. *Revue Française de linguistique appliquée 10*(2), 63–82.

Johnson, T. M., H. R. Solbrig, D. C. Armbrust, and C. G. Chute (2005). Lexgrid editor: Terminology authoring for the lexical grid. In *AMIA 2005, American Medical Informatics Association Annual Symposium, Washington, DC, USA, October 22-26, 2005*.

Kenter, T., T. Erjavec, M. v. Dulmin, and D. Fišer (2012). Lexicon construction and corpus annotation of historical language with the cobalt editor. In *Proceedings of the 6th Workshop on Language Technology for Cultural Heritage, Social Sciences, and Humanities*, LaTeCH '12, pp. 1–6.

Khan, F., F. Boschetti, and F. Frontini (2014). Using lemon to model lexical semantic shift in diachronic lexical resources. In *Proceedings of the Workshop on Linked Data in Linguistics 2014 (LDL-2014)*.

Lenci, A., N. Bel, F. Busa, N. Calzolari, E. Gola, M. Monachini, A. Ogonowski, I. Peters, W. Peters, N. Ruimy, M. Villegas, and A. Zampolli (2000). Simple: A general framework for the development of multilingual lexicons. *Journal of Lexicography 13(4)*, 249–263.

Mel'čuk, I., A. Clas, A. Polguère, et al. (1995). Introduction à la lexicologie explicative et combinatoire. Duculot, Paris/Louvain-la-Neuve.

Mensching, G. (2004). Per la terminologia medico-botanica occitana nei testi ebraici: le liste di sinonimi di shem tov ben isaac di tortosa. *Atti del Convegno internazionale Giornate di studio di lessicografia romanza: il linguaggio scientifico e tecnico (medico, botanico, farmaceutico e nautico) fra Medioevo e Rinascimento (Pisa, 7-8 novembre 2003), Pise, ETS*, 93–108.

Mensching, G. (2009). Listes de synonymes hébraïques-occitanes du domaine médico-botanique au moyen âge. *La voix occitane. Actes du VIIIe Congrès Internationale d'Études Occitanes 1*, 509–526.

Núria Bel, Sergio Espeja, M. M. and M. Villegas (2008, may). Coldic, a lexicographic platform for lmf compliant lexica. In *Proceedings of the Sixth International Conference on Language Resources and Evaluation (LREC'08)*, Marrakech, Morocco. European Language Resources Association (ELRA).

Piccini, S., A. Bellandi, and G. Benotto (2016). Formalizing and querying a diachronic termino-ontological resource: the Clavius case study. In *Proceedings of the Workshop Digitization to Knowledge, July 11, 2016, Krakow, Poland*, Number 126, pp. 38–41.

Piccini, S. and N. Ruimy (2015). Plotiterm: Une ressource termino-ontologique du vocabulaire plotinien. In A. Bozzi (Ed.), *Digital Texts, Translations, Lexicons in the Web*. Firenze: L.S. Olschki.

Pustejovsky, J. (2006). Towards a generative lexical resource : The brandeis semantic ontology. *Proc. LREC 2006*, 385–388.

Reymonet, A., J. Thomas, and N. Aussenac-Gilles (2007). Modelling ontological and terminological resources in owl dl. In *Proceedings of ISWC*, Volume 7.

Ringersma, J. and M. Kemps-Snijders (2007). Creating multimedia dictionaries of endangered languages using LEXUS. In *Proceedings of Interspeech 2007. Baixas, France: ISCA-Int.Speech Communication Assoc.*, pp. 65–68.

Roche, C. Le terme et le concept : fondements d'une ontoterminologie. *TOTh 2007 : Terminologie et Ontologie : Théories et Applications, Jun 2007, Annecy, France*, 1–22.

Romary, L. (2001). An abstract model for the representation of multilingual terminological data: Tmf-terminological markup framework. In *TAMA 2001*.

Schandl, T. and A. Blumauer (2010). *PoolParty: SKOS Thesaurus Management Utilizing Linked Data*, pp. 421–425.

Stempel, W.-D., C. Kraus, R. Peter, and M. Tausend (1997). *Dictionnaire de l'occitan médiéval: DOM: Supplément*. Niemeyer.

Szymanski, J. (2009). Wordventure – developing wordnet in wikipedia-like style.

Tiepmar, J., C. Teichmann, G. Heyer, M. Berti, and G. Crane (2014). A new implementation for canonical text services. In *Proceedings of the 8th Workshop on Language Technology for Cultural Heritage, Social Sciences, and Humanities (LaTeCH)*, pp. 1–8.

Weingart, A. and E. Giovannetti (2016). Extending the lemon model for a dictionary of old occitan medico-botanical terminology. In *International Semantic Web Conference*, pp. 408–421.

Designing an Ontology for the Study of Ritual in Ancient Greek Tragedy

Gloria Mugelli
Università di Pisa
gloria.mugelli@gmail.com

Andrea Bellandi
ILC, CNR Pisa
andrea.bellandi@ilc.cnr.it

Federico Boschetti
ILC, CNR Pisa
federico.boschetti@ilc.cnr.it

Anas Fahad Khan
ILC, CNR Pisa
fahad.khan@ilc.cnr.it

Abstract

We examine the use of an ontology within the context of a system for the annotation and querying of ancient Greek tragic texts. This ontology in question results from the reorganisation of a tagset that was originally used in the annotation of a corpus of tragic texts for salient information regarding ritual and religion and its representation in Greek tragedy. In the article we discuss the original tagset as as providing examples of the annotation. We also describe the structure of the ontology itself as well as its use within a system for querying the annotated corpus.

1   Introduction

In this article we look at the use of an ontology as part of a system for annotating and querying ancient Greek tragic texts[1]. This system was designed to support the research carried out by the first author on the dramatic function of religious ritual in ancient Greek tragedy including an analysis of the utilisation of ritual actions by tragic authors in developing tragic plots. In order to carry out this research it was necessary to create a corpus of annotated texts with the annotation taking into account the most salient phenomena from ancient Greek religion as well as the characteristics of ancient Greek rituals. As background here it is important to consider the fact that religion was embedded into every facet of everyday life in Ancient Greece[2] and that Greek tragedy was primarily a ritual and religious phenomenon[3]. Tragedies were performed during the Great Dionysia, a major Athenian festival dedicated to Dionysus which involved the mass participation of all Athenian citizens together with metics (resident strangers) and strangers[4]. Tragic authors could, then, count on the ritual competences of their audiences when it came to constructing their plots: since, having been involved throughout the year in various public and private religious events, the audience of Greek tragedy had both a ritual memory[5] as well as various ritual skills, including the ability to perform rituals themselves[6]. Studying the dramatic form and function of ritual in Greek tragedy is therefore a matter of analysing the similarities and the differences between the rites as they were performed or described in ancient Greek tragedy, and the actual rituals, as they must have been known by 5th century audiences.

---

[1] The project Euporia, Rituals in ancient Greek tragedy, is carried on by the Laboratorio di Antropologia del Mondo Antico (University of Pisa) and the CoPhiLab of the Institute of Computational Linguistics at the CNR in Pisa, see http://www.himeros.eu/euporiaRAGT/ for details.

[2] See Parker (2005, 2011).

[3] On the relationships between ritual and ancient Greek drama see the long debate between Winkler and Zeitlin (1990); Friedrich (1998); Seaford (1998); Scullion (2002) and the discussion in Graf (2006). See also Calame (2017).

[4] On the dionysiac festivals see Pickard-Cambridge (1968) and the sources collected in Csapo and Slater (1994). On the participation at great public festivals in Athens see Parker (2005).

[5] On the role of memory in ancient Greek ritual see Chaniotis (2006); Taddei (2010).

[6] On the composition and the behavior of the tragic audience see Loscalzo (2008); Roselli (2011). On the competences of the audience in general see Revermann (2006); on the ritual competences of the public of Greek tragedy see Taddei (2014).

The corpus chosen for the annotation comprised all 33 surviving plays by Aeschylus, Sophocles and Euripides, although it does not yet include any of the fragments. The annotations were carried out by the first author (a specialist in the field) using specialist annotation software and with a tagset which she specifically devised for the purpose. The annotation software, known as Euporia, was developed through the adoption of a user centred design based on the annotation practices of classicists. Euporia allows the user to annotate continuous and discontinuous passages of various lengths, and deals with textual and interpretive variants[7]. It is then possible to perform queries on the annotated corpus, searching for all the occurrences of one hashtag or the co-occurrences of two or more hashtags[9]. Once the tragic corpus had been annotated, it became clear that restructuring the tags in the tagset into an ontology would make the annotated corpus even more useful and allow more complex and expressive queries to be made against the text. We will discuss the design of this ontology in section 3, while in the next section we will look in more detail at the original tagset itself.

2 The Design of the Original Tagset

The most representative category in the tagset is that of actions and ritual actions, these include ritual acts (such as sacrifices, supplications, libations, lamentations) but also parts of rituals (such as gestures, movements, speech acts). In order to facilitate research on rituals in their dramatic form, the annotation had to take into account two different types of problems: the dramatic and scenic conventions, and variations from actual ritual norm. Not all kinds of rites were meant to be directly performed on the ancient Greek theater stage: although some ritual actions were extremely well suited for the tragic performance (lamentations, supplications, funerary rites) others, above all animal sacrifice, were never represented. However, even if they were excluded from direct representation on the tragic stage, sacrifices were still very common in tragic plots, and established interesting dynamics between scenic and extra-scenic space: so that for instance characters are imagined performing sacrifices in some distant ritual space (for example a character exits to perform a sacrifice or enters and says he has just finished sacrificing). At the same time, sacrificial rituals performed outside the visible scenic space are discussed, ordered, described, and prepared onstage; sometimes sacrificial objects are even directly carried onstage: for example, a character coming back from a sacrifice may enter the scene wearing his sacrificial robe.

In the annotation of the text, these dynamics are represented with combinations of hashtags that marks not only the mention of a ritual in the texts, but also the characteristics of that ritual, and its relationship with the dramatic performance and with the ritual norm. Two macro categories of tags are used for this purpose: the tag *#s* is used to mark actions, objects, people that are directly represented onstage. On the other hand the tag *#h* is used to mark all the ritual actions that are performed in the context of the tragic plot and perceived as real by the tragic characters. For example, the sequence of the three tags *#h #s #supplicatio* marks the representation of an actual supplication carried out onstage, while the sequence *#h #sacrificium* marks an actual animal sacrifice that is not represented onstage[10].The simple occurrence of the tag *#sacrificium* marks the mention of a sacrifice, one that is not necessarily performed in the tragedy. The tag *#h* is used to isolate the actual ritual events from all ritual discourses. Descriptions and prescriptions on rituals, preparations of rites or discussions on ritual efficacy are extremely relevant to research on the dramatic forms and functions of rituals: they can underline the aspects of a ritual that

---

[7]The passages are annotated with Latin keywords expressed as hashtags[8]. The Latin language makes the tags more concise and precise; the choice was also made for reasons of compatibility with *Memorata Poetis* (www.memoratapoetis.it) a project for the annotation of themes and motifs in Greek, Latin and Arabic epigrams. *Memorata Poetis* combines a top-down approach (with a Latin taxonomy of an index of *rerum notabilium*), and a bottom-up approach, with unstructured tags that are organized in an ontology in a second phase of the work, see Khan et al. (2016).

[9]The prototype version of the search engine (EuporiaSearch) is available at the address http://www.himeros.eu/euporiaRAGT/. The user can enter up to three different keywords: for example a query on the three tags #sacrificium, #victima and #bos retrieves all the passages in which an ox is the victim of a sacrifice: Aesch. *Ag.* 1169; Aesch. *Prom.* 531; Aesch. *Sept.* 276; Eur. *Andr.* 1134; Eur. *El.* 811; 813; 816; 1143; Eur. *Hipp.* 537; Eur. *IA* 1081, 1082, 1113.

[10]The absence of the tag #s simply marks that something is not represented onstage. When a ritual is performed offstage, the tag #extra_scaenam/offstage is added in the interests of clarity.

are important in the development of the plot, and that would likely have been noticed by the audiences of Greek tragedies.

In the next section we look at an example of an annotation from a particular tragedy in order to clarify certain aspects of the annotation as well as illustrating the dynamics between scenic and extra-scenic spaces, and the importance of rituals (real rituals, fake rituals and ritual discourse) in the tragic plot.

3 Iphigenia among the Taurians: a case study

Euripides' *Iphigenia among the Taurians* is one of a number of tragedies related to Agamemnon, the commander-in-chief of the Greeks during the Trojan war, and his descendants, his daughter Iphigenia and his son Orestes. Iphigenia is the eldest and the unluckiest of Agamemnon's children. She is sacrificed by her father, before the expedition at Troy, to appease the gods (Artemis in particular). Iphigenia's sacrifice has two different versions in Greek tragedy, differing in the representation of Iphigenia's attitude[11]. In *Iphigenia among the Taurians*, Euripides represents a different ending for Iphigenia's story: the young girl is secretly saved by Artemis and carried to the land of Taurians. In Tauris, Iphigenia become a priestess of Artemis, in charge of human sacrifices. The play represents Orestes arriving in Tauris where he risks being sacrificed by his sister. Just before the sacrifice, Iphigenia and Orestes recognize each other, after which they finally escape from Tauris and return to Greece. In this tragedy, Euripides represents various different rituals[12]. Setting the play in a remote and barbarian land allows him to initiate a discourse between standard and irregular ritual practices, regarding in particular animal and human sacrifice[13] .

Even if human sacrifices have never been attested in 5th century Athens[14], Greek tragedies describing mythical human sacrifices are very likely to preserve important pieces of information about the actual animal sacrifice: descriptions of irregular ritual practice may have been modeled, by the tragic authors, on the actual ritual experiences of their audience[15]. Various human sacrifices are mentioned in Euripides' *Iphigenia among the Taurians*. The following examples will help to clarify both our bottom-up approach, and the possibilities that the ontology offers to perform queries on the database of the annotations.

In the prologue, Iphigenia describes her sacrifice, explaining why she is still alive and what is she doing in Tauris. The tag *#h* marks the ritual as a real one, since the sacrifice of Iphigenia is supposed to have been performed before the events of the tragic plot took place .

[24 καί μ' Ὀδυσσέως τέχναις...29 Ἀχαιοῖς] #h #virginem_sacrificare

Afterwards, Iphigenia makes several mentions of her duties as a priestess in Tauris, and the human sacrifices of strangers she is used to perform. None of these passages are marked by the tag *#h*, since they do not refer to a specific event: they describe the Taurian ritual practice – abnormal and barbaric for the audiences of Greek tragedy – of sacrificing any strangers who arrive in the land.

When Orestes arrives *incognito* as a stranger, he is the perfect candidate for being sacrificed by his sister, who actually gives the order to prepare the ritual. Here, the annotation marks the fact of giving instructions (*#praecepta*) to prepare a human sacrifice (*#ritum_parare #hominem_sacrificare*).

---

[11]In Aeschylus' Ag., Iphigenia is trying to escape the sacrifice, while in Euripides' IA she ultimately consents to being sacrificed. The willingness of the (animal) sacrificial victim is a very debated question among the specialists of ancient Greek sacrifice.

[12]On ritual practices in Eur. IT see Taddei (2009).

[13]See Bremmer (2013).

[14]In 5th century Athens animal sacrifices were performed on a great number of ritual occasions, see Detienne and Vernant (1979); Van Straten (1995); Ekroth (2002); Parker (2005, 2011); Naiden (2013); human sacrifices instead have never been attested in ancient Athens, although at the same time they are very common in mythical narratives, and are often represented in literary sources, and in Greek tragedy above all, see Bonnechere (1994); Bonnechere and Gagné (2013); Nagy and Prescendi (2013)

[15]A common tragic ritual pattern is the so-called perverted sacrifice: in the tragic texts various homicides described using sacrificial metaphors, see Zeitlin (1965); Henrichs (2004, 2012).

When Orestes and Iphigenia find out the truth about their respective identities, they hatch a plan to escape from Tauris and return to Greece: first of all, Iphigenia has to pretend that the sacrifice is impeded by Orestes' pollution, so that they can reach the seaside for a fake cathartic ritual and escape by sea.

Neither Orestes' sacrifice nor the cathartic ritual are actual rituals within the context of the tragic plot: they are explicitly fake by the characters, and have the function to carry out the tragic plot. At the same time, the two fake ritual have interesting features that can be compared with both the rites actually performed in the tragedy and the actual ritual practice.

When it comes to set out for the cathartic ritual, for example, Iphigenia arranges onstage a procession with Artemis' statue, torches, ritual objects. The procession also escorts the tied Orestes and the lambs whose blood is going to be used in the cathartic ritual. The annotation marks all the details of the sacrificial procession and the fact that we are dealing with a simulation (***#ritum_simulare***) of a procession (***#pompe***) going to a purificatory rite (***#lustratio***).

Eur. IT 1222-1225

1222 τούσδ’ ἄρ’ ἐκβαίνοντας ἤδη δωμάτων ὁρῶ ξένους
1223 καὶ θεᾶς κόσμους νεογνούς τ’ ἄρνας, ὡς φόνῳ φόνον
1224 μυσαρὸν ἐκνίψω, σέλας τε λαμπάδων τά τ’ ἄλλ’ ὅσα
1225 προυθέμην ἐγὼ ξένοισι καὶ θεᾷ καθάρσια.

I see the strangers coming out of the temple now, and the ornaments of the goddess and the new-born lambs, because I will wash blood-pollution away with blood, and the flash of torches and all the rest that I have set out as purification for the strangers and the goddess.

[1222 τούσδ ...1233 θεά] #s #ritum_simulare #pompe #lustratio
[1222 τούσδ˜ξένους] #s #xenos #victima
[1222 τούσδ ...1233 θεά] #s #statua
[1223 νεογνούς τ’ ἄρνας] #s #agnus #victima #aetas
[1223 θεᾶς κόσμους] #s #instrumenta_ritus #kosmos
[1224 σέλας τε λαμπάδων] #s #taedae

4 From the textual annotation to the ontology

Organising the hashtags in the annotation tagset in an ontology enhances the usability of the tagset and allows more complex and expressive queries to be carried out on the annotated text. Furthermore the creation of ontological entities for mythical and dramatic events and characters allows users to integrate their textual annotations with further pieces of background knowledge: this strategy makes it possible to carry out queries that are based both on that which is explicitly stated in the text as well as on other background information about the events themselves which has been added to the ontology[16].

For the design of the ontology a 'bottom-up', a posteriori approach was adopted[17]: we organised the hashtags from the original tagset in classes and subclasses[18], and worked upwards creating new superclasses. We also created object properties to express the relationships between different classes. It is important to point out here that the first author's (our domain expert) knowledge of ancient Greek drama and religion was crucial for reorganising the tagset, and that various other specific issues explored in her research were also taken into consideration during the reorganisation. A large number of the elements in the tagset refer to ritual practices or actions performed during rituals.

---

[16]For a similar approach see Khan et al. (2016)

[17]The bottom-up approach was described at the Göttingen Dialog in Digital Humanities 2016 (http://www.etrap.eu/ activities/gddh-2016/), the proceedings of which are forthcoming.

[18]Although classes are usually expressed with character strings that begin with a capital letter, and properties with strings that begin with a lowercase letter, we chose to preserve the conventions of the tagsets used in the annotation: individuals and classes are expressed, in our ontology, in lowercase and are marked with a sharp (#). The properties we created to establish relationships between classes are expressed in lowercase.

With the purpose of organising the different ritual actions included in the original tagset, we created in the ontology the superclass *#actus* (action) and its subclass *#ritus* (ritual action), along with several other subclasses referring to different types of action: gestures, speech-acts, movements.

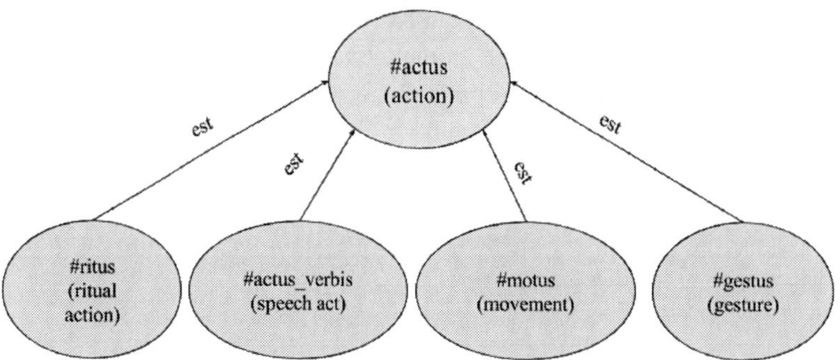

Figure 1: Actions and ritual actions.

Rituals can be characterised by one or more of the categories of actions: a prayer, for example, is a rite (and falls therefore under the *#ritus* class) that also falls under the speech-act class. At the same time, a ritual can involve one or more different sub-actions, annotated in the original tagset. We chose to express the relationship between the different sub-actions performed during a rite and the ritual action itself by creating the property *habet_actum* (has sub-action). The property *habet_actum* (has sub-action) marks an action for the involvement of one or more sub-actions: e.g., a prayer involves the gesture of outstretched-hands.

Creating the superclass *#actus* (action) and the property *habet_actum* (has sub-action) allowed us to model complex ritual practices (ex. sacrifices), that can be divided in phases and can involve a large number of sub-actions. The most important sub-action of a sacrificial ritual, for example, is the ritual killing of the victim; all of the other sub-actions performed within the context of a sacrifice can be divided into two phases, pre-killing and post-killing, during which different types of actions are performed. During the pre-killing phase, for example, the participants are arranged around the altar and the *sacrificant* sprinkles the altar with water and utters a prayer. This phase of the sacrifice therefore involves different sub-actions: a specific position, a gesture and a speech-act.

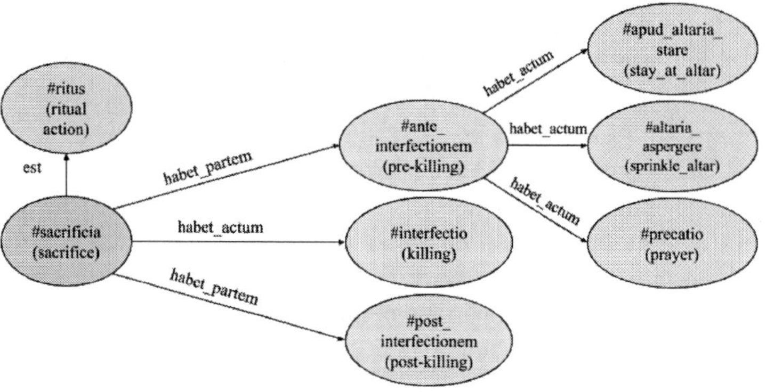

Figure 2: Sacrifice description.

When modelling the classes of ritual actions and actions in general, we had to take into account the problem of ritual agency, that is extremely important for the study of rites and religion. The textual annotation already included hashtags marking the different roles that can be performed during a ritual action, such as *#ritum_agens* (ritual agent) or *#recipiens* (recipient). In our ontology, we chose to model the ritual roles as classes, and we created the correspondent properties (using the latin verb corresponding to the roles) to describe the relationships between the ritual actions and their agents or recipients. A

#ritum_agens (ritual agent) is defined as the class of every individual who *agit* (performs) some *#ritus* (ritual action) and a *#recipiens* (ritual recipient) is defined as the class of every individual who *recipit* (receives) some *#ritus* (ritual action).

We also used the properties *agit* and *recipit* and their inverse properties (*agitur* and *recipitur*) to create axioms that describe the relationships between specific ritual actions and their specific agents or recipients: sacrifices, for example, are always dedicated to gods. We used the property *recipitur* (is received by, inverse property of *recipit*) to state as an axiom that sacrifices have only recipients in the subclass *#deus_recipiens* (recipients-gods): *#sacrificia* ⊑ *recipitur* ONLY *#deus_recipiens*. The subclass is therefore defined as a subclass of both the class *#dei* and *#recipiens*.

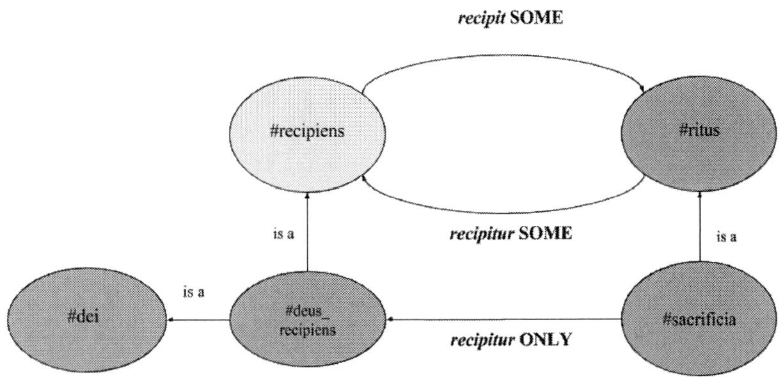

Figure 3: Sacrifices and recipients.

In a sacrifice the role of the victim is of course very important, and it is expressed in our ontology by the class *#victima* (already included in the textual annotation). In actual ancient Greek sacrificial practice this victim was usually an animal. However, our interest in the portrayal of rites in Greek tragedy means that we have to include human sacrifices in our ontology, with sacrifices of virgins as a special case. We defined three types of sacrifice (*#sacrificia*[19]) based on the type of victims they required, specified via the *habet_victimam* (has victim) property. An animal sacrifice has victims only in the subclass *#victima_animalis* (animal victim), a class that is defined as the intersection of the *#victima* (victim) and *#animal* classes; the victims of a human sacrifice only belong to the class of human victims (*#victima_humana*) which latter is represented as an intersection between the class *#victima* and the class *#homo*(human being); finally, a virgin sacrifice is a human sacrifice that has a victim in the subclass of virgins (a subclass of the *#homo* class).

Our ontology can be used to add another layer of salient information pertaining to the tragic texts. Each character in a specific text is represented as an individual in the ontology, however characters can also have different variants across different myths or across different variations of the same myth, and it is useful to model this as well. Indeed myths are naturally subject to variation, and tragic plots represent mythical narratives as well as, at the same time, creating different variants of a myth. In order to give a stable identity to variant versions of the same character we decided to create new individuals, belonging to the class *#heros*, that represent a mythical 'pattern' or 'prototype' for a given character. We link instantiations of characters in an individual text with this so called mythical identity via the property *#est_persona* (is character of)[20]. We have adopted the same approach in creating single ontological events for the mythical or dramatic ritual events.

In Eur IT, we modelled four events as ontological individuals:

---

[19]In the ontology, we used the plural *#sacrificia* to mark the superclass of sacrifices (both animal and human). The singular and unmarked term *#sacrificium* was used in the textual annotation to mark the most common sacrificial practice (animal sacrifices) and it is therefore used in the ontology for the subclass of animal sacrifices.

[20]The annotation included the names of tragic characters only when they were relevant in the understanding of ritual actions (for example when a tragic character is a ritual agent). In our ontology we chose to include an individual for each of characters represented in a play, linked to the corresponding individual in the class *#heros*.

1. The sacrifice of Iphigenia, that is an individual of the *sacrifice of a virgin* class of events, performed by Agamemnon and that has Iphigenia as a victim;

2. The Taurian practice of *human sacrifices* that is a class of events, in particular a subclass of the human sacrifice type. This type of ritual has (human) strangers as victims, and is performed in Tauris by the priestess of Artemis, a role played by Iphigenia in the Euripidean tragedy;

3. The fake sacrifice of Orestes, that is an individual event belonging to the ***#ritum_simulare*** class, that enacts a human sacrifice of the ***taurian_sacrifice*** type. The fake sacrifice has Orestes as a victim, and Iphigenia (in her role of Artemis' priestess) as the ritual agent.

4. The fake purification of the human victims, enacted in the context of the fake human sacrifice.

Points 3 and 4 stress the difference between the actual rituals (marked with the tag ***#h***) and actions that involve rituals (for example simulations, ritual discourses, ritual prescriptions or the preparation of a ritual). The class ***#ritum_simulare*** includes all fake rituals, and can be used to study the function of this dramatic mechanism in the tragic plot. The relationship between a simulated rite and the actual rite is represented by duplicating the ontological events referring to the ritual: we have an individual of the ***#ritum_simulare*** (fake_a_rite) class representing the simulation, and an event of the ***#ritus*** type representing the object of the simulation. The relationship between the simulation and the simulated rite is expressed via the property ***agitur_in_aliquid*** (has object). The duplication of the ontological events stresses the differences between the fake and the real rituals (a fake ritual is not a subclass of *#ritus*). One of the most interesting differences between real and fake rituals is their purpose (***#ritus_propositum***): in the case of the fake purification, for example, we can distinguish between the purpose of the purification (the purity of the sacrificial victim) and the intention of the fake ritual (the escape of the two characters).

By creating single ontological individuals representing specific events we can gather together all the textual mentions of the same event, so that users can easily collect all the different information included in the annotation for a single ritual event. This makes it possible to study how a mythic ritual (the sacrifice of Iphigenia, for example) is represented in different tragedies. It also makes it possible to analyse all the patterns of action involving a ritual in a specific tragedy: in Eur. *IT* the sacrifice of Orestes is firstly recommended and prescribed, then refused, finally simulated by Iphigenia. Moreover, including the ritual events in the ontology allows the user to add (and retrieve) some additional pieces of information about the specific individuals of his/her ontology.

4.1   Using the Ontology to Query the Tragic Corpus

One of the main characteristics of the system which we are currently constructing, and of which the ontology and the annotated corpus are parts, is its close relationship with the tragic text: so that users are able to retrieve information, based on an expert textual annotation, that is useful for anyone interested in the details of Greek tragic texts. And thanks to the ontological component of the system, users can perform queries on both the textual annotation and the ontological events (and their textual occurrences).

Our system prototype is depicted in Figure 4. In order to interact with the corpora itself we use our ontology to create SQL queries according to an original query posed by a user. This original query can be formulated in SPARQL. However accessing structured data in the form of ontologies requires training via a language like SPARQL can incur a significant overhead for users. This is why we feel that it is important to provide a Natural Language Interface that assists in the making of queries (step 1 of Figure 4). Afterwards a specific component maps the query into SPARQL in order to retrieve the right entities (step 2 and 3 of Figure 4). At this level the system can exploit the inferred knowledge by making an expansion of the original query in order to generate a list of SQL queries accordingly (step 4 and 5 of Figure 4). Finally, the data is retrieved by means of Euporia search engine that performs the queries, the results of which are rendered to the scholar by the system GUI (step 6 and 7 of Figure 4).

An example should clarify. Thanks to the fact that the relations between the different type of sacrifice and the different types of agents have been defined, users can perform queries on the ritual features of

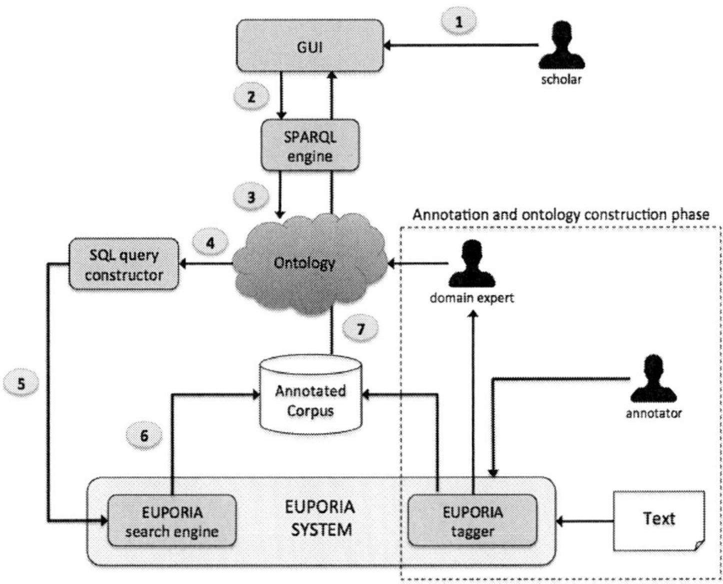

Figure 4: System prototype architecture.

both human and animal sacrifices: so that it's simple to write a query that retrieves, for example, all the female goddesses who receive sacrifices in Greek tragedy. In the textual annotation, the tag *#recipiens* is used to mark the gods receiving a sacrifice, in association with their names whenever their names (or identities) are explicitly stated in the text. For the example query mentioned above the system generates a list of SQL queries in order to retrieve all the cases where the name of a goddess (an individual of the subclass *#dea, female_goddesses*) is annotated in the role of *#recipiens* in the context of a sacrifice, that is one of the subclasses of the *#sacrificia* superclass, including animal sacrifices, human sacrifices and sacrifices of virgins. The results listed below are examples of passages resulting from the different queries:

1. Eur. El. 756: a sacrifice to the nymphs (#sacrificium + #recipiens + #nymphae);

2. Eur. Hel. 1585: a sacrifice to Poseidon and the nereids (#sacrificium + #recipiens + #nereides);

3. Eur. IT 456: the taurian sacrifices of strangers dedicated to Artemis (#hominem_sacrificare + #recipiens + #artemis);

4. Eur. IT 6-9: Iphigenia's sacrifice to Artemis (#virginem_sacrificare + #recipiens + #artemis)[21].

5 Conclusions

In this article we have discussed the use of an ontology as an aid in the study of ritual and religious facts in Greek tragedy. Starting out with an annotated corpus of ancient Greek tragedies we looked at the tagset could be reorganized as an ontology in order to better query the annotated text. This bottom-up approach was adapted to the methodology adopted by the original research on the tragic texts: on the one hand the textual annotation preserves the complexity of the dramatic texts, and allows the retrieval all the ritual-related passages in Greek tragedy; on the other hand the ontology structures the annotations in a way that takes into consideration both ancient Greek ritual norms and the dramatic mechanisms of ancient Greek tragedy. Finally we described an overall system for studying annotated texts in which the

---

[21]Gods and goddesses' names mentioned in tragedy were marked in the annotation, and were then included in our ontology. The domain specialist also asserted informations about the gender and the status of the gods (creating, for example, the class of virgin goddesses) and the family and marriage relations between different gods.

ontology is a component. In future work we plan to create a user friendly interface to our system and as well as looking into how to improve its usability more generally.

Our system offers many possibilities for the study of ritual in Greek tragedy and of ancient Greece in general. Due to the fact that it was designed to consider both religious and dramatic problems, it has a special focus on the comparison of different ritual practices to their literary and dramatic representation. However, the dataset and the ontology should be easily reusable in other projects with a literary or historical scope. Indeed the part of the ontology representing tragic and mythical characters was specifically designed in order to be reused in studies on Greek myth: we represent mythical and tragic characters in a way that allows integration with other mythical variants. In particular the part of the ontology representing ancient Greek rituals can be reused in a comparative perspective. It can be used to compare different aspects of ancient Greek religion and different ways to represent rituals in various sources, being integrated with other similar projects. Finally, the ontology can be used in a broader perspective, to establish comparison between the ancient Greek ritual norm and ritual practices from different civilisations.

References

Bonnechere, P. (1994). *Le sacrifice humain en Grèce ancienne*. Number 3 in Kernos. Suppléments. Athènes Liège: Centre Int. d'Etude de la Religion Grecque Antique.

Bonnechere, P. and R. Gagné (2013, June). *Sacrifices humains Perspectives croisées et représentations*. Liége: Presses universitaires de Liège.

Bremmer, J. (2013). Human Sacrifice in Euripides' Iphigeneia in Tauris: Greek and Barbarian. In R. Gagné and P. Bonnechere (Eds.), *Sacrifices humains. Perspectives croisées et représentations*, pp. 87–100.

Calame, C. (2017). *La tragédie chorale. Poésie grecque et rituel musical*. Paris: Les Belles Lettres.

Chaniotis, A. (2006). Rituals between norms and emotions: ritual as shared experience and memory. In E. Stavrianopoulou (Ed.), *Ritual and Communication in the Graeco-Roman World*, Number 16 in Kernos Supplément, pp. 211–238. Liège.

Csapo, E. and W. Slater (1994). *The Context of Ancient Drama*. Ann Arbor: The University of Michigan Press.

Detienne, M. and J. Vernant (1979, September). *La cuisine du sacrifice en pays grec*. Paris: Gallimard.

Ekroth, G. (2002). *The Sacrificial Rituals of Greek Hero-Cults in the Archaic to the Early Hellenistic Period*. Kernos suppléments. Liége: Presses universitaires de Liège.

Friedrich, R. (1998). Everything to Do with Dyonisos? Ritualism, the Dionysiac, and the Tragic. In M. S. Silk (Ed.), *Tragedy and the tragic : Greek theatre and beyond*, Clarendon paperbacks, pp. 257–283. Oxford: Clarendon press.

Graf, F. (2006). Drama and Ritual. Evolution and Convergences. In E. Medda, M. S. Mirto, and M. P. Pattoni (Eds.), *Komoidotragoidia : intersezioni del tragico e del comico nel teatro del V secolo a.C.*, Number 6 in Seminari e convegni, pp. 103–118. Pisa: Edizioni della Normale.

Henrichs, A. (2004). "Let the Good Prevail": Perversions of the Ritual Process in Greek Tragedy. In D. Yatromanolakis and R. Panagiotis (Eds.), *Greek Ritual Poetics*. Cambridge (Mass.): Harvard University Press.

Henrichs, A. (2012, March). Animal Sacrifice in Greek Tragedy: Ritual, Metaphor, Problematizations. In C. A. Faraone and F. S. Naiden (Eds.), *Greek and Roman Animal Sacrifice: Ancient Victims, Modern Observers*. Cambridge University Press.

Khan, A. F., S. Arrigoni, F. Boschetti, and F. Frontini (2016). Restructuring a Taxonomy of Literary Themes and Motifs for More Efficient Querying. *MATLIT: Materialidades da Literatura 4*(2), 11–27.

Khan, A. F., A. Bellandi, G. Benotto, F. Frontini, E. Giovannetti, and M. Reboul (2016). Leveraging a Narrative Ontology to Query a Literary Text. *OASIcs-OpenAccess Series in Informatics 53*.

Loscalzo, D. (2008, April). *Il pubblico a teatro nella Grecia antica*. Bulzoni.

Mugelli, G., F. Boschetti, R. Del Gratta, A. M. Del Grosso, A. F. Khan, and A. Taddei (2016, December). A User-Centred Design to Annotate Ritual Facts in Ancient Greek Tragedies. *Bulletin of the Institute of Classical Studies 59*(2), 103–120.

Nagy, A. A. and F. Prescendi (2013). *Sacrifices humains : dossiers, discours, comparaisons actes du colloque tenu a l'Université de Genève, 19-20 mai 2011*. Number 160 in Bibliothèque de l'École des hautes études. Turnhout: Brepols.

Naiden, F. S. (2013). *Smoke signals for the gods : ancient Greek sacrifice from the Archaic through Roman periods*. Oxford [etc.]: Oxford University Press.

Parker, R. (2005). *Polytheism and Society at Athens*. Oxford.

Parker, R. (2011). *On greek religion*. London Ithaca: Cornell University Press.

Pickard-Cambridge, A. W. (1968). *The Dramatic Festivals of Athens*. Oxford.

Revermann, M. (2006). The Competence of Theatre Audiences in Fifth- and Fourth-Century Athens. *Journal of Hellenic Studies 126*, 99–124.

Roselli, D. K. (2011, June). *Theater of the People: Spectators and Society in Ancient Athens*. Austin: University of Texas Press.

Scullion, S. (2002, July). 'Nothing to do with Dionysus': tragedy misconceived as ritual. *The Classical Quarterly (New Series) 52*(01), 102–137.

Seaford, R. (1998). Something to Do with Dionysos - Tragedy and the Dionysiac : Response to Friedrich. In M. S. Silk (Ed.), *Tragedy and the tragic : Greek theatre and beyond*, Clarendon paperbacks. Oxford: Clarendon press.

Taddei, A. (2009). Inno e pratiche rituali in Euripide: il caso dell'Ifigenia tra i Tauri. *Paideia* (LXIV), 235–252.

Taddei, A. (2010). Memory, Performance, and Pleasure in Greek Rituals. In A. Chaniotis and L. Silke (Eds.), *Ritual Dynamics and the Science of Ritual*, Volume II, pp. 87–108. Wiesbaden: Harrassowitz Verlag.

Taddei, A. (2014). Le Panatenee nel terzo stasimo degli Eraclidi (Eur. Heracl. 748-783). *LEXIS*.

Van Straten, F. T. (1995). *Hierà Kalà : Images of Animal Sacrifice in Archaic and Classical Greece*. Number 127. Leiden: Brill.

Winkler, J. J. and F. I. Zeitlin (1990). *Nothing to do with Dionysos : Athenian drama in its social context*. Princeton, N.J: Princeton University Press.

Zeitlin, F. I. (1965). The Motif of the Corrupted Sacrifice in Aeschylus' Oresteia. *Transactions and Proceedings of the American Philological Association 96*, 463.